Bedtime Stories For Kids 30 Day Challenge: 30 Days Of Guided Meditation & Fantasy Stories To Help Toddlers& Kids Fall Asleep, Relax Deeply, Develop Mindfulness& Bond With Parents

Mindfulness Meditations Made Easy

Table of Contents

The Most Uncomfortable Bed in the World........... 2

The Elf With Incredibly Large Ears 10

The Most Beautiful Places in the World 16

The Baby Bird Who Fell From Her Nest 22

The Unicorn Who Lost His Tail............................ 29

The Mermaid Who Couldn't Swim 36

The Four Little Pigs 43

The Princess and the Prince 49

The Trees Throw a Party 56

The Nice Dragon 62

The Wrong Potion 69

The Bee Who Loved All of the Flowers 75

Uncle Ron Babysits 81

When Aliens Attack 88

The Trapped Fairy 95

The Boy With No Birthday.................................. 101

The Baby That Could Not Sleep........................ 108

The Weird Guy... 115

How To Calm Your Mind 120

The Musical Animals 126

- The Oil Fountain 133
- The Most Beautiful Flower In The World 140
- The Labyrinth 146
- The Story Of Sleep 152
- From Red To Green 159
- The Wind 165
- When The Moon Disappeared 170
- The Luckiest Boy In The World 177
- Survival 183
- The Angry Crocodile 189

INSTRUCTIONS FOR AUDIO RECORDING: 20 MINUTES PER STORY FOR A TOTAL OF 10 HOURS.

THANK YOU!

The Most Uncomfortable Bed in the World

Once upon a time, there was a little girl. Her name was Alice, and she was four years old. The thing that she loved to do more than anything in the world was to sleep. When bedtime came, she would curl up in her bed as her mom and dad read her a bedtime story, and she would slowly fall off to sleep.

Well, she wouldn't slowly fall off to sleep. First, she would have to make herself comfortable, for her bed always seemed to turn into the most uncomfortable bed in the world as soon as she tried to make herself comfy.

"Are you comfortable?" asked her mother.

"I think so," said Alice.

Her mother opened the book and began to read the story of the elf with the big ears. She had only just read the first sentence, which was 'Once upon a time, 'when Alice started to squirm in her bed.

"Are you okay?" asked her mother.

"There is something in my bed," said Alice. She wriggled around like a wriggly worm, flipping her legs back and forth as if she was as uncomfortable as she could get. Finally, she could take it no longer, and she jumped out of bed to try and solve the problem. Her mom and dad helped her to find what was bothering her.

"Perhaps it is a rusty, old nail," said her father.

"Maybe there are some rocks in your bed," suggested her mother.

The three of them searched through the bed from top to bottom and almost came up empty-handed. It was Alice who found the culprit.

"Aha!" she shouted as she held her and aloft. Her mother and father had to come closer to see what she was holding. There, between the tip of her index finger and her thumb, was a small piece of brown fluff. It was barely the size of a pea, and we all know that anything the size of a pea cannot make you uncomfortable, but it did make Alice uncomfortable.

Her mother and father frowned, but they were glad that the annoyance had been found, and, when Alice was back in bed, her mother once again started to read about the elf with big ears.

"Once upon a time," started her mother.

"Ouch," said Alice.

"My goodness, what is wrong now?" asked her mother.

"The mattress is sticking into me. I think that there is something wrong with it, maybe a spring is loose," complained Alice.
"Let's call your father to help," suggested her mother.

When her father came, they took the blankets and pillows from the bed, removed all of the stuffed toys (of which there were a lot), removed the sheets, and looked at the mattress. Alice's father conducted a thorough examination of the mattress, checking every square inch. He got in close so that he could examine the fabric, he ran his hand over the surface to make sure that nothing was sticking out, and he pushed down on the springs to check that they were still springy. They were.

"Looks fine to me," he said.

"Have you checked the other side?" asked Alice.

Her father frowned, but he knew that his daughter would not go to sleep until she was comfortable. They already had everything off the bed, so it would not take much more effort to check the other side of the mattress. When he lifted the mattress, Alice saw the problem immediately.

Under the mattress was a shiny, green pea. Alice picked it up and smiled. "This must have been bothering me," she said.

Her mother frowned and took the pea from her daughter. She knew better than to question how a pea could cause so much discomfort.

"Perhaps there is another fairytale that we can read," suggested her mother, inspired by the discovery of the small pea under the mattress.

"No, I like this one," smiled Alice.

The three of them worked to put everything back on the bed. The sheets were tucked in, the stuffed animals were put back in place, the blankets and pillows were laid on top, and Alice got back into bed.

"Are you comfortable now?" asked her mother.

"Oh, yes!" exclaimed Alice.

"Good," said her mother. She restarted the story of the elf that had large ears. "Once upon a time."

Alice fidgeted under the blanket, pulling it up around her neck, and then pushing it down to her chest. She flopped her arms in top of the blanket, and then stuck them underneath it. She moved her head from side to side on her pillow and sighed.

"Are you sure that you are okay?" asked her mother.

"Completely fine," said Alice.

"Okay. Once upon a time," started her mother.

"Hmph," said Alice.

"Once upon a time," said her mother.

"Hmm," sighed Alice.

"Once upon a time," whispered her mother.

"Grr," said Alice exasperated.

"You're not fine, are you?" asked her mother, even though the answer to that was an obvious one.

"I don't mean to complain," said Alice.

"Of course not," agreed her mother.

"But, there is something wrong with this blanket. And the pillowcase," stated Alice.

"And, what is wrong with them?" asked her mother.

"They are too rough," said Alice. "I don't know if you've switched fabric softener, or if I have been sleeping on them for too long, but they are very uncomfortable, and I am not one to complain. "

"Yes, you never complain," agreed her mother. "I thought that something like this may happen, so I have a backup set of sheets and blankets. They are fresh out of the dryer. Would you like to help me put them on?"

"Oh, yes," smiled Alice. "If we change the sheets, pillowcase, and blankets, I am sure that I will sleep soundly.

So, Alice and her mother set to work. They took everything off of the bed, and Alice's mother muttered something about how they should have done this when they were checking the mattress. They replaced the sheet with a new warm, fluffy one, switched the blanket for one that was much softer, and replaced the pillowcase with one that was not so rough.

Alice jumped back into bed and snuggled into the warmth. Alice's mother sat and watched her daughter, waiting for any sign of discomfort.

"You can begin the story, Mother," stated Alice.

One more time, Alice's mother started the story of the elf who had incredibly large ears. "Once upon a time."

Alive kicked the blanket up into the air and let it flutter back down on top of her.

"Once upon a time," said Alice's mother again.

"Whew," whispered Alice.

"Once upon a time." Alice's mother tried to start the story again.

Alice wiped her brow with an exaggerated motion.

"Are you okay?" asked her mother. "Are you not comfortable?"

"No, I am," said Alice. "I mean, the blankets and sheets are comfortable, but they are very warm."

"Warm?" asked her mother.

"Yes, warm," repeated Alice. "They are just out of the dryer and still very warm. Would you mind opening the window a little? But not too much or I will get too cold, and not too little or I will stay warm and be unable to sleep."

Her mother walked to the window, opened it a crack, and let some of the cool breeze trail into the room.

"How is that?" she asked.

"Just right," said Alice.

"So, can we continue with the story?" asked her mother.

"You know," said Alice. "It is getting late, and I am very tired. Maybe we can try to read the story again tomorrow night."

"Yes, tomorrow night," agreed her mother. One of these days they would get past the first line of the story. "Goodnight."

"Goodnight," said Alice. She got herself comfortable and fell fast asleep.

The Elf With Incredibly Large Ears

Once upon a time, there was an elf born with incredibly large ears. When he first appeared, his ears were of average size. Average for an elf, anyway. You see, elf ears are larger than human ears, and they are a little pointed at the top. So, if a human baby was born with elf ears, they would look very big in comparison to human ears. When this elf was born, his ears were the regular size for elf ears.

But, as he grew, his ears did too, and not in a normal elf-ear way. They grew faster than they should and showed no signs of stopping. When he was one-year-old, his ears were the same size as a four-year-old elf's. And, when he was four-years-old, his ears were the same size as an adult elf's. When he turned seven-years-old, his ears were bigger than any other elf's in the village. Even bigger than old-elf-McGonnoggogal, who had the elf record for the biggest ears in the village. (He also had the biggest ears in the elf world, he just did not know it). Well, he *had* the biggest elf ears in the world, all until Bosco turned seven.

When Bosco turned seven, he held the record for having the biggest elf ears that had ever been seen. You would think that this would be something to be proud of, but Bosco was far from proud. In fact, he was a little ashamed of his ears. His large ears brought him a lot of attention, and he did not like that. He wanted to keep to himself and live a simple life, but other elves would not let him.

There were even some who teased him about his ears. Some of the other elves compared him to an elephant, which was not a very accurate comparison. While his ears were large in size, they were not shaped like an elephant's ears. Elephant ears are big and round. While Bosco's ears were big, but they were not round. They stuck straight up in the air and were pointed.

Now, think about your ears. They sit nicely on the side of your head. You are probably happy with the size of them. They are large enough that they don't look weird and small enough so that they don't look extra weird. Now, stick your arms straight up in the air. That is how high Bosco's ears stretched. You can imagine how much of a nuisance that was.

Bosco tried to hide his ears. He would cover his head with large hats, but you need an extra-large hat to cover ears that size. He tried tying them to his head, folding them over, and taping them to the top of his head. That worked for a while, but they would always spring up again. He tried not to go outside, but that was impossible to do. There are so many things to be done outside. Just think of all the things you do outside. There are way too many things to be done to stay inside every day of your life.

"I guess I will just have to accept them," said Bosco.

"Yeah, that's the spirit," shouted Largo. Largo was Bosco's best friend, and he was enthusiastic about everything. Today, they were finally turning sixteen, and that meant they could join the elf army.

The elf army did not do much. They helped other elves build homes, directed traffic when needed, and rescued cats from trees. Yes, there are cats in the elf kingdom. They also wage war with the birds. Every so often, the birds attack, and the elves fend them off.

If you have ever had a bird poop on you, you know how awful that can be. Now, imagine if you have ten thousand birds, and they are all pooping on your village. That is exactly what the elf army faced. When the birds came, they would bang pots and pans together to scare the birds away, but not before the birds had pooped a lot.

Then, the cleanup would begin. You can imagine how awful it is to have to clean bird poop from every house in your entire village, not to mention cleaning up any that fell on the heads of unsuspecting people.

There was one time that they saw the birds coming, but that had been pure luck. No, they just had to deal with it when they arrived.

Bosco and Largo were at the signup for new recruits, and it was not going well for Bosco. While he was the right height and fitness level for the elf army, he could not put on his army hat. His ears were just too big. Finally, they had to cut holes in the hat so that he could wear it.

Next came the obstacle course. That went fine for the most part, but when it came to crawling under the chicken wire, Bosco got his ears caught, and he got stuck. It took three other elves to get him out.

They practiced with paintball guns next. It was a lot of fun to run around and shoot each other with paint, but Bosco was hit more than any other elf. His ears stuck up so much that he could not hide in any bushes or trees. When the day was done, he looked like a rainbow, but he did not feel like one.

"I'm sorry," said the elf general. "I love your enthusiasm, but you are just not cut out to be in the army, Bosco."

"I understand," said Bosco. And, he truly did. His ears had held him back a lot in his life, and this was just another way that they were getting in his way, literally and figuratively.

As he left the elf army compound, he could hear some of the new recruits laughing at him. He was used to that too, and ignored them. As he went home, he knew that he would never be able to help against the bird attacks. He sat in his room and stared out of the window.

"I know that I can help if I am just given a chance," he said to himself.

Bosco sighed and tried to think about what he could do to help, but there was nothing. His ears had gotten in the way again.

With one final push, his ears grew another inch. They had finally reached their full size. No elf had ever had bigger ears, and no elf would.

Bosco sighed again, and a weird sound traveled to him. It sounded like birds. Bosco looked out of the window but could not see any birds. He listened again and was sure that he could hear the squawking of a thousand birds.

He rubbed his ears and knew for sure that the bird squadron was approaching.

Bosco ran as fast as he could to the elf general. He told the general what he had heard. The general believed him immediately. Bosco was not an elf who told lies.

The troops were mobilized. The elf army grabbed their weapons, their pots, pans, and large wooden spoons and began to bang them as loudly as they could.

It was four minutes before the birds appeared.

When the birds got close, the banging noise startled them, and they turned tail and fled. Not one part of the elf village was pooped on that day.

From that day forth, Bosco became the lookout elf, but instead of looking for the birds, he listened for them. Never again was the elf village caught unprepared, and never again were the houses and people covered in bird poop.

The Most Beautiful Places in the World

Have you ever thought about how beautiful the world is?

When you think about it, the world is a marvelous place. There are wonderful things in the world, some that were discovered long ago, some that were discovered recently, and some that have not yet been discovered.

Let's start with an undiscovered place.

Have you ever been swimming, dipped your feet into the ocean, or even just gone underwater in the bathtub? How deep have you swum?

No matter how deep you have gone, you have never gone as deep as the deepest part of the ocean. Do you know how I know that? Because no one has gone there. There are some places in the ocean that have never been seen.

The deeper you go into the ocean, the weirder things start to get. Do you know that there are some sea creatures that live so deep that they are completely blind? There is no light down there, so why would they need to see? There are also fish that can create their own lights, like little flashlights on the top of their heads.

What do you think you would find if you were to dive down to the deepest part of the ocean?

Some people think there are mermaids down there or whole civilizations! I bet there are weird sea creatures down there. Maybe there are starfish with thirty points, or whales bigger than the blue whales, or large dolphins that can talk. What do you think is down there?

Let's move away from the ocean and climb the tallest mountain. Mount Everest is very tall. When you are standing up there, you are as close to the moon as you can get without flying. You can't touch it, though, it's still too far up in the sky.

But, you can look out at the beautiful mountains before you. And, people have been to the top of Mount Everest before, so we know what it looks like up there. The mountain is covered in snow, and that looks very beautiful. The air is also very thin up there, so it is harder to breathe.

I bet there are lots of birds up there. There are lots of clouds too. What shapes do you think they make? Maybe some look like bunnies, and some look like butterflies. Do you think you could see your home from up there? If you were at the top, would you shout something and see how it sounded?

Okay, it's time to come down from there. You cannot live up there. There are no houses, and no food to grow. It's very cold too. I hope that you are tucked up in bed, all nice and warm.

Where shall we go next?
How about on a Safari?

In Africa, there are large patches of land that have lots of cool animals. You could walk through the plains of Africa by yourself, but I wouldn't recommend it. There are lots of wild animals there. Better to fly over in a small plane or drive through in a jeep.

If you spend enough time there, you might see lions and tigers and elephants and meerkats and rhinos and hippos and giraffes and colorful birds. If you could be any of those animals, which one would you be? If you could watch one of those animals, which one would you like to watch?

While we are close, why don't we visit the pyramids!

The pyramids are very cool and were built a long time ago. Some people think that aliens built the pyramids, but it was probably the ancient Egyptians, the people who lived in Egypt. There are still Egyptians in Egypt, but they are not ancient. Some are the same age as you, and some are the same age as your parents or grandparents.

Pyramids are square on the bottom and have triangular sides. Each side meets with the others at a pointy top. They are very big. Think about how big your house is or how big the biggest house is that you have ever seen. The pyramids are a lot bigger.

They also have secret rooms and treasures. If you ever find yourself stuck in a pyramid, don't forget to look for those secret rooms, and you might find some of that treasure.
Where else can you find treasure?

Pirates used to find and hide treasure. They would bury treasure on islands, and draw maps so that they would not forget where they had hidden it. There are no pirates anymore, but there might be some treasure buried on an island somewhere.

Maybe there is some on the island that is far away from everyone. There is one island in the middle of the ocean that is very far away from any people. It is so far away that it is closer to people in space than people on Earth. When the space station passes over, the astronauts inside are closer to the island than any other people on Earth. How cool is that? I bet there is treasure buried there.

Volcanoes can be beautiful too, but don't get to close to them. They are very hot and can erupt at any moment. It is cool to see volcanoes erupt in the ocean. They can't hurt anyone, and sometimes they create new islands. If there were pirates now, I bet that they would hide their treasures on those islands.

What about places where there is no water?

The Sahara desert is like a giant sandpit, except you would have to walk for months to get out of it, if you got lost there. And there is not much water there. But that doesn't stop people from living there. If you know where to look, you can find water. Some is hidden under the ground, and some is hidden inside plants like cactuses.

It is not the best place to live, but it is very beautiful, with sand that stretches as far as the eye can see.

The Antarctic desert is considered the largest desert in the world. This is kind of funny as it is not made from sand but from snow and ice. A desert is a place where it does not rain very much, if at all. That is why the Antarctic is still a desert. It may have lots of snow, but it doesn't rain.

Do you think that you could live there? Snow and ice are very beautiful, but they make it hard to live. You could build an igloo, and that would keep you warm, but food is hard to get, you couldn't just go to the grocery store.

Okay, that is enough of that. I bet that all the talk of snow and ice is making you cold. This is supposed to be a bedtime story that makes you feel all cuddly and warm, not one that makes your toes icy cold.

Let's imagine that your bed is in the desert. As you pull your blanket up over your body, imagine the warm sun beating down on you. If you have a cuddly toy, cuddle up to it. If not, imagine you are cuddling with a stuffed animal, one from the safari.

Wriggle your toes, because that is always fun, and close your eyes. There are so many beautiful places in the world, and you may get to discover one of them when you are older. For now, you can visit them in your dreams.

If there is a place that you would like to visit, imagine that place now. Hold the thought in your mind as you drift off to sleep, and you might just dream about it. If you would like to visit a place in your own imagination, imagine that place in your mind and hold into it as you fall asleep.

Now, lay back, relax, and let your dreams come.

Goodnight.

The Baby Bird Who Fell From Her Nest

There once was a baby bird. This baby bird could not yet fly, but that was okay, for she had a safe nest to live in with her mama and daddy.

One blustery fall day, when Daddy Bird and Mama Bird were out looking for food, Baby Bird was looking out across all of the trees in the forest.

Suddenly, a large gust of wind ripped through the trees and shook the nest. But, Baby Bird did not fall out. She looked out over the trees and smiled as they swayed in the wind.

Another gust came, stronger than the previous one, and shook the tree ferociously. Baby Bird held on with her tiny claws and was glad that she did not fall out.

"I am never going to fall out of this tree," she exclaimed.

Just then, right as she said it, the biggest gust of wind ever felt, passed through the branches. It rustled leaves, ruffled feathers, and rumbled as it moved across the land. You would think that Baby Bird would have been blown from the nest, but she was not.

She laughed at the wind, and did a little dance, flapping her wings. That was when she tripped and fell from the tree.

Down, down, down she went. She flapped her wings, but she could not yet fly. Her talons reached out and gripped a vine. She held onto the vine and swung in a large arc. Through the forest she went until she hit a baby tree. She held onto the tree and slipped down it. Baby Bird hit the ground with a small thump.

Baby Bird squawked. She was well and truly lost. When she looked around, she could not see her mama and daddy, she could not see her nest, and she could not see her tree. She had never left her nest before, and it was a little scary.

"Hello."

Baby Bird turned around in shock. She was not sure what to expect and had definitely not expected to see a tiger standing there. She had read about tigers in books but had never met one before. It looked like a large pussy cat, and she was sure that it was just as tame.

"Are you lost?" asked the tiger.

"Yes," said Baby Bird. "Will you help me to find my tree?"

"Of course," said the tiger, for this was a very helpful and charming tiger. Exactly the kind of tiger that you

would invite to tea, if you had a lot of food to be eaten and tea to be drunk.
"Hop on my back." said the tiger. He bent down so that the baby bird could hop up onto his back.

Baby Bird got on and was impressed with how soft the tiger was. As soon as she was on his back, he gave a soft growl and began to walk through the forest.

"Is that your tree?" asked the tiger.

"No, that tree is an oak tree. I live in a silver birch tree. The leaves are the wrong shape," replied Baby Bird.

" How about that tree?" asked the tiger.

"Is the bark silver?" asked Baby Bird.

"No," said the tiger.

"Then that is not the tree," said Baby Bird.

"How about that one?" asked Tiger.

"No," replied Baby Bird.

"That one?"

"Nope."

"That one?"

"No, not that one."

"That one?"

"Definitely not that one."

"How about that one?"

"Look," said Baby Bird. "You need to keep asking me the same question when we pass every single tree."

"But that one has silver bark," said the tiger. "I thought that it might be your silver birch tree."

"Oh, yeah," said Baby Bird, a little embarrassed. "That does look like my tree. Okay, Tiger, up you go."

"What?" asked the startled tiger. "I can't climb trees. I'm a tiger. We are very suited for the ground, thank you very much."

"Well, what am I to do?" asked Baby Bird.

"I can take you."

Baby Bird looked up and saw a monkey hanging in the tree above. He swung back and forth before jumping and doing a somersault through the air, landing on his feet beside the tiger and Baby Bird.

"You really will take me up the tree?" asked Baby Bird.

"Yes, I will," said the monkey with a cheerful smile. "Hop onto my back and hold on tight."

Baby Bird did as she was told. She hopped onto the monkey's back and held on tight to his fur. As soon as she was on, the monkey took off. She did not even have time to say goodbye and thank you to the tiger as they climbed up through the trees.

The monkey was fast and lithe. He gripped a branch, pulled on it, swung on another with his tail, and could reach the next branch up. Baby Bird had expected the monkey to stop at every nest, but he kept going, up and up. Soon it was all a blur to Baby Bird, and she could not make out anything.

But, one thing that she knew for sure was that the nest was at the top of the tree, so she did not say anything to the monkey.

Then, as fast as they had set off, they stopped. Baby Bird looked up and could see her nest only a few meters from where they were.

"That is it," laughed Baby Bird.

"Yes, there is it," said the monkey. "There is only one problem."

"What is it?" asked Baby Bird.

"I cannot go any higher," answered the monkey. "I am much too fast, and the branches are swaying too much. If I go higher, I am afraid that I will fall."

"Well, how am I supposed to get up there?" asked Baby Bird. "I cannot fly, and I cannot climb."

"I...can...help."

Baby Bird looked up and saw a sloth.

"I...can...take...you...up...there," said the sloth very slowly. In fact, Baby Bird almost fell asleep as the sloth talked.

"Oh, thank you," said Baby Bird.

It took the sloth four minutes to get from the branch that he was on to the branch below. When he got there, he scooped up Baby Bird with his long toes and continued the journey upwards. The going was slow, for sloths are very slow creatures.

It took the sloth one minute to pick up Baby Bird, two minutes to introduce himself, and six minutes to plan the route to the top, which was only a few branches away.

They moved so slowly that Baby Bird did fall asleep and would have fallen back to the ground if the sloth was not holding her so tightly.

Baby Bird woke up when the sloth needed to scratch his nose. That took the sloth nine minutes, and then he had to scratch his ear, which took a further eight minutes. From where the monkey had departed to the nest was only two meters, but it took the sloth three hours to get there.

When Baby Bird was safely back in the nest, she did not care. She was home, and she was safe.

"Thank you," said Baby Bird.

"You...are...welcome," said the sloth. That took fifty seconds to say.

The sloth left, and Baby Bird looked out for her mama and daddy to return. It was not long before they did, and Baby Bird danced a dance because she was so happy. As she danced, she tripped and fell from the nest.

Thankfully, Daddy Bird caught her and placed her back in the nest.

"That was close," he said. "You almost fell to the forest floor. You cannot imagine what you would find down there.

Baby Bird hugged her mama and daddy and was happy.

The Unicorn Who Lost His Tail

Many years ago, there lived unicorns. This was back when magic was still alive. There were elves and fairies too, but they are not important to this story, so we are not going to mention them anymore.

There was a short time when unicorns and humans lived together, but that did not last very long before the magical world and the real world separated. This story takes place long before humans were around, and concerns a unicorn by the name of Francisco.

Francisco was a beautiful unicorn. He had grey hair, but not a dirty grey. It was a shiny, clean grey that was luxurious and soft. His mother helped him to brush it every day, and that kept it so soft and lustrous. He also had a silver horn. He was particularly proud of his horn and polished that every day too. It shone like a star.

But, more glorious than his coat and his horn was his tail. Francisco's tail was a rainbow of color. Each strand of hair was a different color and, when it swished, it almost looked like a rainbow shining in the sky.

Francisco loved his tail more than anything in the world, so he was very upset one morning when he woke up and found that his tail was missing. He was sure that he had it the day before, but he could not remember where he had put it.

"Mom! Have you seen my tail?" he shouted.
"Have you checked under the bed?" shouted his mom from downstairs.

"Geez, Mom, of course I have. That was like the first place that I looked," said Francisco.

"Well, keep looking," suggested his mom.

"Obviously," said Francisco. He was a little annoyed at having lost his tail and didn't think that his mom was being helpful.

"But, it is my tail," said Francisco to himself. "I was the one who lost it, so I should be the one to find it."

Francisco tried to think what he had been doing the previous evening, but he had done so much that he did not know where he had left his tail. He decided that he would just have to look everywhere for it.

"I'm going out, Mom. I'm going to go and look for my tail," said Francisco.

"Don't be long," said his mom. "I'm making blueberry pancakes for breakfast.

Francisco loved blueberry pancakes, so he vowed to make the search quick. He ran out of the house, feeling weird without a tail, and searched all over the unicorn kingdom.

The first place he went to was the volatile volcano. He had been there last night, but it was a lot calmer then. He stepped around the edge of the volcano and peered in. As he did, the volcano erupted, and Francisco had to jump back so that his hair was not singed.

Francisco was a very agile unicorn and had amazing balance, but this was a test, even for him. He carefully clip-clopped around the mouth of the volcano. It erupted five more times, and each time he managed to dodge the fiery lava. When he had walked around the mouth of the volcano six times, he decided to search elsewhere. His tail was not in the volcano.

Next up was the dragon cave. Dragons and unicorns are great friends, but not in the early morning. Dragons like to sleep late, and they can be very grumpy if you wake them too early. When Francisco arrived at the dragon cave, the largest and grumpiest dragon was sleeping at its edge.

Fransisco knew better than to wake that particular dragon, so he went into stealth mode. Stealth mode involved standing on the edges of his hooves and stepping extremely lightly.

First, he snuck up to the dragon to make sure that he actually was asleep. Next, he tip-toed past (or tip-hoofed past), heaping an eye on the dragon the entire time. The dragon's chest continued to rise and fall, and small wisps of smoke escaped from its nose.

When Francisco was inside the cave, he was even quieter for any sound would reverberate around the stone cave walls and create even more noise. Francisco searched everywhere that he could think of, but came up empty-handed. The tail was not there.

Next up was the land of the witches. He had been there recently, and his tail could have slipped off.

"Have you seen my tail?" asked Francisco.

"Perhaps," said the oldest witch. "If you can answer me these three riddles, I will tell you where I saw it."

"Okay," said Francisco.

The witch asked the three riddles. Now, these riddles are so difficult that there is no point in recording them here, for they would only succeed in driving your crazy and melting your brain.

Francisco thought long and hard. He had always liked puzzles, but these riddles were extra difficult. He used all of his brainpower, thinking through each one, and he finally came up with three answers.

"Red. The mole was made of ice. Seven-thousand-and-seventy-six," said Francisco.

"Exactly correct," said the witch.

"So, now you will tell me where you saw my tail?" asked Francisco.

"Yes," replied the witch. "I have not seen it anywhere."

Francisco was disappointed. The last place to look was the land of the giants. If his tail was going to be anywhere, then surely it would be there. There was only one problem.

The entrance to the land of giants had been blocked by a landslide. The large arch that usually led to the giant kingdom was blocked by large rocks that had fallen from the mountains above. Francisco set to work.

He moved some of the smaller blocks, using his unicorn strength. He turned the larger blocks and kicked them with his solid hooves, then moved the smaller pieces. It took him a long time, and he started to become hungry, salivating at the thought of the blueberry pancakes that were at home.

When the work was finally done, a large giant approached.

"Hey, thanks for clearing that, I was just coming to do that myself," said the giant.

"Have you seen my tail?" asked Francisco with hope.

"No," said the giant. He walked away.

There was nowhere else to look, and Francisco turned and walked home. If he had a tail, it would have hung low, but he did not have a tail. Instead, he hung his head.

When he got home, the smell of blueberry pancakes was wafting through the house, but he was not in a mood to eat them.

"Did you find it?" asked his mom.

"No," replied Francisco sadly.

"Did you check under your bed?" asked his mom.

"Yes, Mom! I already told you that. Geez, do you think that I am stupid? Look, I'll go and do it again. I've checked under there like three times, but I guess it will magically appear under there if I look again," whined Francisco.

He stomped angrily up the stairs and looked under his bed.

There it was!

That was when he remembered that he had not actually looked under his bed. He smiled to himself, then frowned to himself, then laughed to himself. He wondered if this whole adventure had taught him a lesson.

"Probably not," he murmured.

Francisco went downstairs to find his mom at the kitchen table, serving up pancakes. She glanced at Francisco's magnificent tail but did not say a word. Instead, she served him up some pancakes as he sat down to eat.

Francisco poured some syrup on his pancakes and splashed some on his tail.

Francisco and his mom both laughed.

The Mermaid Who Couldn't Swim

If you have ever read any stories about mermaids, then you know that they are fantastic swimmers. But, mermaids are not born being able to swim, they must learn how to do it, just as you had to learn how to walk.

Now, walking can be tricky, but most people learn how to do it. If you have learned to walk, then well done, and, if not, then you will surely learn how to walk or find another way to get around.

The ocean is a different place, and mermaids cannot get around any other way than swimming. When they are born, they cannot swim, and when they turn three years old, they usually can. Before that age, they are typically strapped to their mothers and carried around or pushed around in large shells.

But, it is widely known that mermaids learn to swim when they are three years old. Well, all except for one.

Aqua was born under a full moon, which is always a sign of good fortune in the underwater world. When she was born, the moonlight was rippling through the water, and a ray of moonshine shone on her head when she first appeared. She looked just like a princess.

But, she didn't act like one. She was very, very, very, very, very, very, very, very stubborn.

She was so stubborn that she did not do anything unless she wanted to do it. That was fine when she was young, but it started to make things a little more difficult when she was older. Especially when she got to three years old.

When she was three, everyone expected her to start swimming. She was stubborn, but that had never held her back. She had always been a mermaid who dreamed big and did everything that she could to achieve her dreams.

Only, it would seem that her dreams did not include swimming.

For the first week after her third birthday, her parents did not think much of it. It was not unusual for some mermaids to start swimming after they were three. The only problem was that Aqua did not even try. She would sit in the sand, not swishing her rich, blue tail, and not going anywhere. And she seemed very pleased with herself.

After a month, her parents started to get worried. Aqua was a healthy young mermaid, but she would not move from her spot in the sand unless she was carried.

"I have an idea," said her mama.

She swam over to Aqua and looked her straight in the eye. "Aqua, I want you to know that I am not going to carry you around anymore. It is time for you to swim by yourself."

"Okay," said Aqua.

Her mama was pleased. When it was time for dinner, her mama called on her and told her that it was time to come home. Aqua said okay, but she did not move. No matter what her mama said, Aqua would not move from her spot. She would not swim.

"Okay, just this one time," said her mama. She picked up Aqua and took her home.

The next day, she was called in for dinner again, Aqua stayed where she was.

" Aren't you going to swim?" asked her mama.

" I'm not ready yet," said Aqua.

"That does not matter," said her mama. "You need to start learning to swim, or you are never going to be able to swim."

This went on for seven more days. Aqua's mama would call her in for food or bath time (yes, mermaids have baths) or bedtime or something else, but Aqua would not swim. Every time, her mama would make an exception and carry her in.

"You are not helping her," said Aqua's father. "Leave this to me, what we need is some tough love."

The family went outside, and Aqua's father told her that they were going to a very special place to play. Aqua asked if she could come, and her father said that she could, all she had to do was to swim with them.

"I don't think that I am ready yet," said Aqua.

"Well, if you don't swim, you won't get to play in this really amazing place," said her father.

"Hmm," mused Aqua. "I do like to play."

"Okay," said her father. "We are going now."

The entire family swam away slowly. They whipped their tails gently, all at the same time, and moved slowly away from Aqua. They pretended to talk about this amazing place they were going to (in actual fact, there was no amazing place. This was all Aqua's father's idea to get Aqua to swim). You can probably guess that it did not work.

The mermaid family hid around the corner and watched. Aqua looked troubled. For a moment, they thought that she was going to swim after them, but she went back to playing in the sand. Aqua's father frowned, but he was not beaten just yet.

He tried again the next day. He told Aqua that they were going for ice cream. There is special ice cream under the water that does not melt like regular ice cream. Aqua loves ice cream, and she was tempted to go with her family, but she was not yet ready to swim.

The next day it was a trip to an underwater volcano, then a weird shark that had a rainbow tail, then a secret cave that may have treasure in it. Aqua was tempted by all of those things, but not tempted enough to do anything about it.

"I know what to do," said Willow, Aqua's sister. "She just needs to see us swimming around her more."

Aqua's parents did not know what to do, and this was their last option, so they agreed.

Willow, and Aqua's two other sisters, swam as much as they could around Aqua.

"Look at us," said Willow. "Look at what we can do. Isn't this cool!"

"Yeah, it's pretty cool," said Aqua.

"Don't you want to join us?" asked Willow.

"When I am ready," said Aqua.

Willow and her sisters swam fast in a line, darting past Aqua trailing a long line of bubbles behind them. They found some dolphins and rode on their backs. They swam in large circles, looping upside down, then around and around. They placed various loops and tunnels and swam through them as fast as they could. They even got a blue whale to agree to help them, and the sisters swam in and out of its mouth.

"Doesn't this look fun?" asked Willow.
"So much fun," agreed Aqua.

Still, she did not swim. Willow and her sisters tried this for an entire month, but Aqua did not move from her spot in the sand.

Six months after her third birthday, Aqua's parents gave up. "I don't think that she is ever going to swim," said her mother.

"Hey, would you look at that," said her father.

They looked outside to see Aqua swimming. Not only that, but she was the most magnificent swimmer that they had ever seen. She streaked past, swimming faster than any other mermaid could. She corkscrewed and twisted. She beat her tail, creating gigantic bubbles. She even swam to the surface, jumped out, did three backflips, and landed gracefully back in the water.

When Aqua swam home, her parents stared at her in disbelief. Their mouths hung open wide, not able to believe what they were seeing. Aqua had not swum for six months, and now she was the best swimmer in the ocean.

Aqua stopped in front of her house and looked at her disbelieving parents. "I guess that I was ready," she said. She swam away to play with her sisters, go to an exciting place, and find some ice cream or treasure.

The Four Little Pigs

Everyone knows the story of the three little pigs, but not many people know the story of the four little pigs, for those three brothers had a sister who ran away to join the circus, and that story is quite amazing. Can you believe that a pig could join the circus? Well, this story is about how all four pigs eventually joined the circus, and the wolf was never really to blame.

Now, in the traditional story, the three little pigs are scared of the wolf, for no reason other than he is not a pig, and they lose their houses. Let's start a little before that.

When the four little pigs first came to Wolfsville, they thought that it was a great place to start a new life. All except for the youngest pig, Geraldina. She did not want to live in a city, and she had tried to convince her brothers to join the circus with her.

The three brothers were afraid of height, did not like clowns, and were terrified of doing anything in front of a crowd.

"This is the life for me," said Abe, the oldest pig.

"Yes, I will be quite safe here," agreed Gabe, the middle brother.

"Oh, yes, a nice city life with a boring job," chimed Babe, the youngest of the three brothers.

So, the three little pigs set up a new life in the city of Wolfsville. Abe found a job as an accountant, Gabe found a job as an accountant, and Babe found a job as an accountant. And, they were all happy, for precisely seven minutes.

Meanwhile, Geraldina joined the circus and did boring circus things like put her head in a lion's mouth, walk the tightrope that was three miles high, juggle nine balls of fire, and clean up the elephant dung. She was happy for precisely seven minutes, and then she was happy for every single minute after that.

But, Geraldina missed one thing. Well, she missed three things. She missed her three older brothers. She sent regular postcards detailing precisely what she had been up to, and she enjoyed hearing from her brothers, even if they talked a lot about accounting.

Back in the city of Wolfsville, the three brothers were starting to grow tired of their jobs. The first seven minutes had been a lot of fun, but they were starting to get tired of numbers. But, the three pig brothers were not ones to give up, so they decided to start building homes. They did not have enough money to stay in a hotel for their entire lives.

This is partly where the original fairytale starts. As you may have guessed, Babe made a home out of straw, Gabe made a home out of sticks, and Abe made a home out of bricks. You are probably thinking that bricks are a suitable material for a home, but why would you build a home out of straw and sticks?

You may be thinking that the pigs did not want their homes to last for a long time, and you would be right. Gabe and Babe were already thinking about moving away from Wolfsville and joining the circus with their sister, but they were a little scared to make that leap.

"Maybe our houses will fall down," suggested Gabe.

"Then we can join the circus," said Babe.

There had been many postcards from their sister, and they were longing for a life without numbers, and with more elephant poo.

There was only one problem. While their houses were made from straw and sticks, they were still well built. They did not want to destroy their own houses, for they were still not sure about joining the circus. They were hoping that something would make the decision for them, and they would have no choice. Pigs can be funny like that.

Thankfully for Gabe and Babe, something did come along. Rather, *someone* came along. Wilfred, the wolf, was a building inspector, and he was in charge of all of the buildings in Wolfsville. After the three new houses were built by the pig brothers, he scheduled a time to come and visit them.

Wilfred was a very nice wolf and was known all around the community as the nice, little wolf. It is astounding, then, that his name was eventually changed to the big, bad wolf. He was never big, and he was never bad.

When he got to Babe's house, he was amazed.

"How can you live in a house of straw?" asked Wilfred.

"I don't know," said Babe.

"This house is going to come down when the first breeze hits it," said Wilfred. To illustrate this, he blew on the house, and the entire house collapsed.

Babe pretended to be sad, but he was secretly happy. He could finally join the circus. He skipped after the wolf as Wilfred went to visit Abe.

When Wilfred got to Abe's house, he was astounded.

"Why would you ever build a house from sticks?" asked Wilfred.

"I don't know," said Gabe.

"You have not even used any glue or tape," said Wilfred. "The first time that an earthquake hits, this house is going to come crumbling down. It is a health hazard."

"I don't know what I was thinking," said Gabe.

To illustrate what an earthquake would be like, Wilfred shook the house gently. The entire house of sticks came tumbling down.

"I'm sorry," said Wilfred.
"That's okay," said Gabe. Secretly, he was happy. He could finally run away and join the circus.

Gabe and Babe followed Wilfred as he went to visit Abe. When Wilfred got to Abe's house, he was pleasantly surprised. He found a well-built house, made of bricks.

"This is a very fine house," said Wilfred. "It will survive wind, earthquakes, and pretty much anything else that you can throw at it."

"Thank you," said Abe. He felt proud but sad at the same time. He wanted to join the circus too, but he was also a sensible builder of houses.

When Wilfred left, the three pig brothers were left alone.

"You can live here with me if you like," said Abe.

"No, we are going to run away and join the circus," said Gabe.

"Yeah, we are done being accountants. We are going to be clowns or trapeze artists or jugglers," said Babe.

"Well, then let's get to work," said Abe. "I can't leave if I have a perfectly good house to live in."

The three brothers set about demolishing the brick house. They used hammers and chisels to remove the bricks. They smashed everything inside, ripped up everything on the outside, and made a really big mess.

When Wilfred returned (he had forgotten his hat), he found a pile of bricks with a hat on the top. He shook his head and was glad that the three funny pigs had left. They were nice pigs, but they were not very good at building houses.

The three little pigs started a new life. They packed what little they had, found the traveling circus, and joined Geraldina. They became the most astounding pigs that had ever been seen. The four of them became expert jugglers, they all walked the high wire at the same time, and they flew through the air as trapeze artists.

The finale of every show involved them each placing their heads inside of a lion's mouth. The crowd would always go wild, and that made the pigs happy. They had been bored as accountants, and they had finally found something that they loved doing.

Of course, they still took care of the circus accounts; they were trained to deal with numbers, after all.

The Princess and the Prince

There once was a handsome prince. He lived in the wealthiest kingdom in all the land. He was tall, had long, flowing golden hair, dressed in the most stylish clothes, wore shiny shoes, treated everyone very kindly, had lots of friends, was very mature for his age, worked hard, had a pet iguana, and longed to find a wife.

He would walk about all day and say things like, "Nice job!" and "You look good today!" and "What a nice person you are!" and "Have some of my ice cream!"

Everybody loved the prince, and the prince loved everybody.

On the other side of the kingdom, there lived a princess. She had long, straggly locks of hair that she never brushed, she liked to wear the same clothes every day, she was kind but shy, had a pet dog (that was very scruffy), often got angry at the injustice in the world, but always wore a smile on her face.

While she could come across as brash, everyone in the castle loved her, because she had a true heart and would always speak the truth, though that sometimes hurt people a little.

She would say things like, "You need to help out more," or "Why are you wearing so many rings?" or "Stop worrying about what people think of you and have some fun," or "I like ice cream."

There is one more character in this story: the big dragon who lives in the mountains. Dragons like to steal helpless people, and I bet that you can guess what happened next. Yes, the dragon flew to the kingdom, swooped down into the gardens, and stole the handsome prince.

Well, the kingdom was in an uproar. That prince had been due to marry a beautiful princess from another kingdom, and the king and queen were very upset.

"I am upset," said the king.

"I am very upset," said the queen.

They decided to do all that they could to save the prince. They assembled all of the soldiers that they had, armed them with the very best weapons, and sent them off to rescue the prince. They returned a few days later with very burnt clothes.

When the princess heard that her betrothed had been captured by a dragon, she was extremely upset.

"I am extremely upset," said the princess.

"I am upset, too," said her father.

"Yes, me too," said her mother.

They decided that if the king and queen of the other kingdom could not save the prince, they would have to do it instead. They were a king and queen too, and they had an army also. They called in all their best knights, equipped them with the very best armor, and sent them to save the prince.

The knights returned a few days later with extremely burned armor, and no prince. They gave up, for there was absolutely nothing that they could do. The prince was lost forever.

Meanwhile, Princess Anastasia, the one with the straggly hair, was brooding in her room. She had not been allowed to climb on the castle roof as it was far too dangerous. Well, she would just have to think of something else.

"Father, why can't I play on the roof?" she asked the next day.

"It is much too dangerous," said her father, who was also a king. There once was a lot of kings and queens in the world.

"Well, I suppose that I will have to find something safer to do," said Anastasia.

"Yes, I suppose that you will," agreed the king.

"Perhaps I will go and fight the dragon so that the prince can be free," suggested Anastasia.

"Yes," agreed her father. "That sounds like a nice way to spend your day, and not at all dangerous."
So, Princess Anastasia gathered some of her belongings, her best leather armor, a sharp steel sword, a large wooden shield, and some food. She left the castle on a horse, munching on an apple as she rode.

It was a long way to the mountains, and there were some obstacles to overcome first. In the wetlands, she had to dismount her horse and lead it through the shallower waters. When they were out the other side, she got back on the horse and rode again.

"Well done, Hamish," said Anastasia. Hamish was the name of her horse.

The jungle was next. Anastasia dismounted again and used her sword to hack her way through large branches and vines. Some of the vines even reached out to grab her, but she was much too quick. There were large spiders too, but they were friendly, and one even came along for the ride.

The quicksand was next. At the edge of the quicksand, there was a sign:

Enter ye, all who dare!
But of the sand, beware, beware!
Once you enter, you don t get out!
No matter if you scream or shout!

Anastasia looked out across the quicksand and thought about what to do. It would be dangerous to go through the quicksand, and she did not want to get stuck. So, she decided to go around. It was not too much out of her way, and it only added three more minutes to her journey.

The swampland was next, and she had to go through that, for there was no other way to get to the mountain. She tread very carefully, guiding Hamish so that he did not get sucked into the swampy mud. At one point, a large swamp monster appeared, but they are deathly afraid of spiders, so it quickly ran away.

After the swamp, they reached the mountains. It was tough going, constantly ascending the steep, craggy rock, but Hamish was an excellent horse, and Anastasia was an excellent rider. When they reached the mouth of the cave, Anastasia dismounted and shouted:

"DRAGON! GET OUR HERE, I NEED TO HAVE A WORD WITH YOU!"

The dragon was there in seconds. Anastasia can shout very loud, and the dragon looked scared when he came out of the cave, but quickly regained his composure when he saw that a princess was standing there.

"Let the prince go!" demanded Anastasia.

"No," said the dragon.

"I thought that you would say that," said Anastasia. "So, I have come prepared to fight. Will you face me?"

"Yes," said the dragon.

The fight began.
The dragon leaped into the air, flapping its large wings, almost pinning Anastasia to the ground. A plume of fire came next, shooting from the dragon's mouth, straight at Anastasia. She managed to roll and dodge the first blast, but the second came all too soon. She blocked it with her shield and could feel the searing heat.

Quickly, she rolled behind a rock and out of sight. She clambered up the cave entrance and positioned herself behind the dragon. While the great beast searched for her, she leaped onto its back and ran up its spine. When she reached the dragon's head, she did a somersault, leaped up into the air, came back down, and bonked the dragon on the nose with her sword.

Tears welled in the dragon's eyes, and it quickly flew away. When the dust had settled, the handsome prince emerged from the cave. He was a little dirty but still looked extremely dashing in his regal clothes.

"Thank you for saving me," said the prince. "I was due to marry another princess, but I will now marry you for being so brave."

"No thank you," said Anastasia. "I have many more adventures to go on, and I cannot yet think about marrying someone. I am much too young."

"Oh," said the prince.

They both went home to their kingdoms, and the prince married the princess that he had been promised to.

Anastasia continued to have adventures until she was ninety-nine. She fought many more dragons, found endless treasure, and even brought peace to the entire kingdom.

The Trees Throw a Party

There are some people who ask the classic question: if a tree falls in the forest, and no one is around to hear it, does it make a sound?

What they should be using is what music do trees like to dance to?

Trees don't often just fall over for no reason, but they do like to dance and do it quite often. When all of the people have cleared out of the forest, and no one is close by to see them, the trees often throw a party.

At this party, there is lots of singing and dancing. Most trees are horrible singers, and you never want to hear a tree sing, but they are the most amazing dancers and, if you ever get to see them dance, you will agree with all your heart.

Once a year, when the Northern Lights are the brightest, the trees throw the biggest party. The animals will often come to visit and watch the trees dance, and if you are a friend of the trees, you might be invited too.

Not many people have seen trees dancing.

The oak trees are always the ones to get the party started. During the day, they stand magnificently in the forest, regal and mighty. They hold acorns in their hands, gifting some to the squirrels for food, and dropping others to the ground to grow more oak trees.

As soon as the Northern Lights are shining, the oak trees start to dance. Their dances are a simple one. They sway from side to side as if they are moving with the wind, but there is no wind, they are dancing. The more they sway, the higher they lift their branches, as if they are trying to touch the stars.

This signifies the start of the dancing party, and all of the other trees join in. The weeping willows are usually next.

Weeping willows have long branches that hang down to the ground. Imagine someone who is crying, with their head and hands hanging down. This is how the weeping willow looks, only as a tree. While weeping willows look sad, they are one of the happiest trees at the party.

When they start to feel the Northern Lights 'music, they bop side to side, as if they are dancing with their shoulders. Of course, trees do not have shoulders, but the dance looks like this.

When they dance, they smile wide and laugh. If you were another tree, you would spot this immediately. If you look closely, you might see it. Their leaves start to quiver, and this is them smiling. Then leaves also make a rustling noise, and this is their laughter. The weeping willows, and the oak trees dance together in time.

The silver birch trees come next, though they have to be careful as birds often nest in their trees. These trees like to breakdance. While the weeping willows and oaks are moving side to side, the silver birch trees move their branches like they are robots.
Some of them, the more experienced dancers, will crouch down and throw their roots out to one side and then the other. If you are lucky, you may see them spin on the forest floor, sometimes on their heads.

The weeping willows always receive massive cheers from the other trees, and this gets the party started, with all of the other trees joining in.

The palm trees are the jokers of the tree worlds. They like to take their own coconuts and bang them together in time with the music of the Northern Lights. They slowly beat their coconuts faster and faster, causing every tree to dance quicker and quicker until their branches cannot keep up, and the trees fall to the floor.

The palm trees laugh but soon help everyone up, and they each find a partner to dance with. They love the old ballroom dances, and will often waltz around the forest with the other trees. If you were to look down on the trees from above, like the Northern Lights can, you would see all of the trees moving together, each with a partner, and each moving in and out of the other.

It is a beautiful thing to see, and the palm trees are amazing dancers, even if they do like to cause mischief.

The baby trees join in next. Once they have seen the adult trees dancing, they want to join in and do the same. They imitate the older trees and hone their dancing skills so that they will be expert dancers when they are older.

Next, come all of the fruit trees from the orchards. None of these trees dance like any other, and they all freestyle dance, doing their own thing, but still following the music. As the other trees are dancing together, the fruit trees weave in and out, and dance in time with those around, but performing dance moves that no other can. This helps to make their fruit even sweeter and delicious for when you get your hands on it.

The sycamore and pine trees like to dance together. When they arrive at the party, they select a partner and dance with that partner for the entire night. They often split into groups of eight, and perform dances together, dancing in jigs or reels, switching partners, but always ending back with their original partner.

It is fun to watch a tree spin back and forth between dance partners, and the sound of the swishing leaves when this happens is unlike anything else that you can imagine.

As the trees dance under the Northern Lights, the colors become rich and vivid. There are greens, blues, purples, reds, and yellows in the sky, colors dancing to their own tune. Down below, the leaves all start as green but soon change to every color of the rainbow.

The greens are too many to count, and, as the trees dance, their leaves change color as if every season is happening at once. Greens become yellows, oranges, reds, browns, blacks, whites, and then green again. The leaves look like an ocean as they all dance together.

More and more trees come from all around, all of them dancing their own dance, and smiling and laughing. This is the most joyous occasion for the trees.

The giant sequoia trees always arrive last. They are so big that it takes them longer than any other tree to get there. They tower above the forest, with thick red trunks that seem to stretch up to the sky. When they come, they start to sing in low booming voices, making the ground tremble. It sounds like a thousand musicians playing tubas, trumpets, and drums, all at the same time.

The trees all come together and sway from side to side in time with the choir of sequoia trees. If you were there, you would feel the entire forest shaking, and you would not be able to stop swaying with the trees.

When the song is done, the trees all leave and return home. As the sun rises, the Northern Lights leave to sleep. The forest returns to normal.

So, the next time you find yourself in a forest and you feel like dancing, please do. The trees love to see people dance and, if you don't tell anyone, they might just dance with you too.

The Nice Dragon

Detrimus is a very common name for a dragon. Meteor is also very popular, and Flame is a not-so-original name that has been passed down through the generations. You will find many Flame Juniors and Flame the thirds. It was confusing then, that Edgar was called Edgar, and he often puzzled over his name.

"Why did you call me, Edgar?" Edgar asked when he was five.

"It suited you," said his mother. "When you were born, you looked like an Edgar."

Edgar had to agree. When he looked at himself in the mirror, he did not look like a Brodgar or a Fireball or even a Smoky. He looked just like an Edgar, so he learned to love his name.

As he lay in bed that night, he forgot all about his name and worried more about starting school. Tomorrow was going to be his first day at dragon school, and he was a little bit nervous about it. He had some friends starting with him (Flame, Flame Jr, and Destroyer), but that did not help to calm his nerves.

When he woke up the next morning, Edgar dressed in his new dragon school uniform, ate his charred pancakes, and walked to school. Thankfully, it was not far. When he got there, he found his friends, and they all went to class together.

The classes were pretty simple, and he was taught English and Math. Even though dragons don't need to write, they do need to read. They need to make sure that the treasure they find is not fake. They also need to read signs so that they know where they are going when they are stealing princesses.

After lunch, how to steal princesses was the next class. They learned how to swoop down, grab a princess, and then hide her in a cave. They practiced outside with watermelons and hid them in trees.

"Why do we steal princesses?" asked Edgar.

"Because they are princesses," said his teacher as if that was an acceptable answer.

"Yes, but why?" asked Edgar.

"Because we have always done it," said his teacher.

"But, why did we start?" asked Edgar.

"Because we are dragons," replied his teacher, giving a smile as if he had just solved a complicated problem.

This did not satisfy Edgar, and the questioning continued for a long time after this until the school bell rang, and it was time to move onto the next class. Edger did not get an answer that he liked.

"Stop being a troublemaker," said one of his classmates, a large red dragon with sharp teeth.
"I'm just trying to be nice," said Edgar.

"Well, dragons are not nice," replied the red dragon.

"Why not?" asked Edgar.

"Because we are dragons," said his classmate. The red dragon walked off as if he had given a satisfactory answer. He had not. Not for Edgar, anyway.

The next class was all about how to find treasure and how to store it. Edgar had to admit that this class was fun. It was like hide and seek but, instead of other dragons hiding, there was gold hidden. The dragons had to search for it, like a treasure hunt or a scavenger hunt.

When all the gold had been found, the dragons stood around it. The large pie of gold was impressive and shiny.

"Why do we hoard treasure?" asked Edgar.

"What kind of a stupid question is that?" asked his teacher. "What else are you supposed to do with treasure?"

"But, we can't spend it or use it," said Edgar.

"No," said the teacher, waiting for Edgar to get to the point.

"Then, why do we hoard it?" asked Edgar again.

"Because it is treasure," said the teacher. He folded his arms as if he had answered all of Edgar's questions, and the young dragon would now thank him for being so wise.

"What if we didn't hoard treasure?" asked Edgar. "What if we did something else. Hoarding treasure is so time consuming and dangerous."

"If we didn't hoard treasure, then we would have no treasure," said the teacher.

"Exactly," said Edgar.

"Exactly," responded his teacher as if they were in agreement.

They were not. Nothing that his teachers said made any sense to Edgar, and they were supposed to be his teachers. What chance did he have in life if he was not going to be able to get answers to any of his questions?

The final class of the day was about fighting knights. The life of a dragon is hazardous, and they are under constant attack by knights.

The dragons learned how to dodge arrows, sidestep swords, and duck under maces. They also learned how to hurl fire and practiced on straw dummies. Edgar had a lot of fun doing this, but he did have some questions.

"Why do knights attack us?" asked Edgar.

"Because we steal treasure and princesses," replied his teacher as if this was the most obvious thing in the world.

"What if we didn't steal that stuff?" asked Edgar. "Isn't stealing bad?"

"Then we wouldn't have that stuff," said the teacher. "Without stealing that stuff, we wouldn't be able to fight so many knights."

"Wouldn't that make it safer to be a dragon?" asked Edgar. "If we didn't steal things that we didn't need, then we wouldn't have to fight knights that we don't have to fight."

"Ah, you are still young," said the teacher. He lowered his voice so that he could whisper. Sometimes adult dragons like to whisper to make what they say seem more important. "It is dragon nature to steal treasure and princesses. That is just who we are. Just as knights like us to steal that stuff as it is in their nature to fight dragons. If we didn't steal, they would have nothing to do. If we didn't steal stuff, we wouldn't have anything to do, and then where would we all be? It's very complicated.

I wouldn't expect a young dragon like you to understand."

Edgar didn't understand it, but it didn't seem complicated. It seemed very simple.

The teacher ushered the students away with a big smile on his face as if he had just solved all of their problems.

Edgar stopped asking questions. While the teachers had a lot of answers, they never really answered what he was asking. He decided to take a different approach. As he grew up, he didn't steal anything and was nice to everyone instead. It took a lot of work for the humans to trust him, but eventually, they did.

Instead of stealing princesses and treasure and fighting knights, Edgar used his skills to move large rocks or fuel furnaces. The world's humans appreciated his hard work and knew that he was different from the other dragons.

They would pay him in food and other useful things, but Edgar still accepted some treasure, as he knew that the older dragons liked that sort of thing. It was very shiny but completely useless.

When the other dragons saw him bring the useful items and useless treasures home, they marveled at how he had collected so much. When he told them that the humans had just given them to him, they did not believe him at first.

The younger dragons joined him on some of his excursions, and they found that they could earn whatever they desired by doing a little work. It was certainly easier than sealing, definitely more fun, and there was a limited threat from knights.

As more and more dragons took up this new life, more and more joined in. Soon, all of the dragons had given up their old life of stealing and were soon working with the humans to help them, and help themselves.

"I knew that I gave you the right name," said Edgar's mother one night as they were sat at home. "You are not a Destroyer, or a Flame, or a Smoky. You are definitely an Edgar."

Edgar could not help but agree.

The Wrong Potion

Agnes was not born with the name Agnes, but when she became a witch, she renamed herself. When she was born, her name had been Petunia Sunflower Witherington. When she became a witch, at the age of sixteen, she renamed herself Agnes Broomstick.

Of course, she did not tell her family that she had become a witch. They would not believe her if she did tell them, so it was best to keep that kind of thing to herself.

Agnes moved to a small wooden shack in the woods, a classic destination for most witches, and told her family that she had moved to the big city to work as a secretary. They were happy that she had a job, and Agnes was happy that she would never have to work in a boring job. Witches have ways of making money, from selling potions to those who believed in witches, to curing ailments that cannot be cured by doctors, to turning bad people into frogs.

Agnes specialized in making potions. In fact, she was one of the best witches around at making potions, even though they sometimes went very wrong.

The potions that she would make could turn people into any animal they wanted, could give you superpowers, and could help your tomato plants to grow more tomatoes.

She had just received an order from a man who needed the boils removed from his face.

"Easy, easy, easy," said Agnes when the man contacted her. "Removing boils is one of the easiest potions in the world."

"Oh, good," said the man. "He had called Agnes from his office and needed the boils to be gone by lunchtime. He had a very important meeting to go to after lunch, where he and his business associates would talk about very boring things that they were very interested in.

"Yes, I will deliver it myself," said Agnes. "Just tell me one thing, how many boils do you have? It is very important to know the exact number so that I can add the exact ingredients."

"I have thirteen boils," said the man.

"AAAAAAAAAAAYYYYYYYYYEEEEEEEIIIIIIIIII!!!!!!!!!" screamed Agnes.

The businessman almost dropped the phone, the scream had been so loud.

"Sorry," said Agnes when she had regained her composure. "Boils are easy, but not so much when you have thirteen of them. That is the worst number of boils that you can have."

"Can you help me?" asked the businessman. There was a lot of worry in his voice, and he was starting to suspect that he would have to skip his important meeting. He held the phone to his ear and waited. It felt like an eternity before Agnes Broomstick spoke again.

"Yes, I can do it," she said.

"Thank you," said the businessman. He hung up the phone and checked himself one more time in the mirror. His face was covered in thirteen big, green boils.

Agnes hung up the phone on her end. She did not have a phone, but she did have a log that she spoke into, so she placed the log back down in its holder.

"This is going to be harder than I thought," said Agnes. "If he had twelve boils, I could whip up a potion in sixty seconds, and if he had fourteen boils, I could have a potion ready in half that time. Thirteen is an unlucky number, and this is going to take some time, but I am sure that I can get it done by lunchtime."

Agnes Broomstick liked a challenge, and this was certainly going to be a challenge. She pulled out her extra-large cauldron from the cupboard and placed it in the middle of her room, directly over the small woodpile. She lit a fire beneath it and got to work.

First, came all of the regular ingredients that make up most witch potions. She added thirteen spider legs, thirteen eyes of newt, thirteen pinches of salt, and thirteen bat wings. As she stirred the potion in large circles, she felt satisfied that the potion making was going well.

"I think that this is going to go without a hitch," said Agnes. "I do not think that there are going to be any problems whatsoever."

Next, came the crucial part. There were two ways that she could go with this potion. She could add the blue food coloring to give the potion a nice blue tint, or the red food coloring to give the potion a nice red tint.

One color would create the correct potion, and the other could end the world. She always got the two mixed up, but was sure that the blue food coloring was the right one. She dumped the entire bottle into the potion and took a step back. When nothing happened, she breathed a sigh of relief.

"Right, as always," she whispered.

She continued on with the potion. She added some lemongrass, one cat hair, some globulous goo, ten sprigs of heather, and a willow wisp. That is when the trouble began. As she added the willow wisp, the potion started to bubble ferociously and let out a large gargled burp. The burp covered Agnes and turned her skin completely green.

This put Agnes in a panic. She was now sure that she had put in the wrong color. She would have to do everything in her power to save the potion. She threw in tree bark, and the potion almost exploded. A dark cloud appeared over her small shack. When it started to rain, it rained cats and dogs. Cats and dogs began dropping from the sky with lots of meows and barks.

To combat this, she added some oregano. That only succeeded in growing the cloud, and it soon covered the entire world, raining cats and doge over the entire planet.

When Agnes added some cocoa powder and essence of frog, everything started to shrink, and I mean everything. Her cauldron, her home, her forest, her country, and the entire planet started to shrink. It would only be a few minutes before it shrank into nothing.

She threw in seven rat tails, which caused everyone in the world to turn into jelly. That would be a problem, but at least the businessman would not have to go to his meeting. When she threw in red berries, all of the water in the world turned into hot chocolate. She added sugar to the cauldron, but that did not help.

Pickles and paprika were added next, and that turned the world inside out. It was still raining cats and dogs, people were made from jelly, all the water was hot chocolate, and the world had turned inside out.

Right before the world disappeared from existence, Agnes threw her watch into the cauldron and stirred it in the opposite direction. Everything reversed, and she was taken back in time. All the cats and dogs were sucked back up into the sky, the world grew back to normal size, people were not jelly anymore, and the water was water again.

Agnes found herself holding the blue and red food coloring bottles, wondering which one to add.
"I guess I should add the red one this time," she said. She dumped in the red food coloring, took a step back, and was happy when it turned a nice pink color. She added the rest of the ingredients and ladled the mixture into a bottle.

It was 11.30 am when she hopped onto her broomstick with the boil-removal potion. She flew quickly to the offices of the businessman and delivered the potion. He quickly uncorked the bottle, drank it all, and licked his lips. As soon as he had drunk it, the boils vanished from his face.

Agnes was glad that he could go to his meeting.

She was also glad that she had not destroyed the entire world.

The Bee Who Loved All of the Flowers

Bees love flowers more than any other creature in the world, even curious little boys and girls, but there is one bee that loves flowers more than anyone else.

Bert is a busy bee. He loves to fly from flower to flower and collect pollen. That pollen is one of the things he loves about flowers. Bert loves that the pollen us turned into honey and that he can share all of that honey with people around the world.

It is a magical transition, and Bert still marvels when it happens. The bright yellow pollen that he collects is turned into yummy honey for people to enjoy.

But that is not the main reason why he loves flowers so much.

He loves flowers so much because every flower is different and every flower is beautiful. Even though some flowers are the same variety, they always have slightly different colors, or the petals are shaped differently; some are short while others are tall, and they even smell different.

Some flowers don't hold the pollen that Bert needs, but he still likes to visit them. He always makes sure to visit all of the flowers so that none of them feel left out. Flowers have feelings too.

The sunflowers are his absolute favorites, and they are always the flower that he visits first. There is a bonus reason as to why he visits this flower first and that it down to their size.

When Bert first wakes up in the morning, much like any bumblebee, he is very tired. I am sure it is the same if you have to wake up early.

When he is still sleepy, it is hard to stay focused when he is flying. That makes sunflowers perfect. They are so tall and big that they are easy to see when it is still early in the morning, and the sun is not yet fully up.

Sunflowers look like mini suns, making them the perfect flower for Bert to visit. They are so easy to see that it is the perfect start to his day. Of course, they are beautiful and magnificent too.

"Good morning, sunflowers," Bert says as he arrives at the sunflowers and hovers in front of them for a while.

Once he has visited them, he plays feels more awake.

Next, Bert visits the orchids. They are a delicate flower, and they come in all the colors of the rainbow. While Bert does not play favorites with the flowers, he would admit that orchids are the most beautiful.

One thing that he likes about visiting orchids in the early morning is that they always match a color that is in the sky. As the sun starts to rise, the sky goes through many different colors, starting as black, becoming more purple, before moving through red, orange, yellow, green, and blue.

As Bert visits the orchids, he can find an orchid to match every color of the sky, and that is a good way to wakeup. As he flies from flower to flower, it gives him his morning exercise, which helps wake him up and get ready for his day.

"Good morning, orchids," Bert says.

Once Bert is ready to start the hard work, he goes straight for the flowers that give the most pollen. The next stop is always lavender. Not only is lavender a great producer of pollen, and perfect for making honey, but it also smells amazing. If you have ever passed under a lavender bush and breathed in deeply, then you will know exactly what I mean.

"Good morning, lavender," Bert says when he arrives at the flower.

Now, he gets to work. He collects as much pollen as he can before he starts to feel sleepy. It is a lot of work to collect pollen. When he has collected enough, it is time to think about a morning nap.

Poppies and tulips are perfect for sleeping in. Bert's favorite color has always been red, and he loves to nap in red petals. Poppies and tulips are very soft too, and perfect for a bee to take a nap in. The flower he chooses will depend on which he is closest to.

"Good morning, tulips," he will say if he chooses tulips and, "Good morning, poppies," he will say if he chooses poppies. "May I sleep in you."

The flowers will always agree because they love to have bees sleeping in them. Bert likes to sleep for forty-five minutes, and he always feels very energized after that. When he wakes up, he goes off in search of bluebells.

Bluebells look like mini street lamps but, instead of having white or yellow lamps on the top of long poles, they have droopy, blue lamps. Bert always feels very sneaky when he has to go underneath the flower and fly up into it. He feels like a bee ninja who is stealing the pollen, though he never actually steals it, the flowers want him to have it.

"Good afternoon, bluebells," Bert says.

When he is done with the bluebells, it is time to have a little fun. It is time to visit the dandelions.

First, he lands on the bright yellow dandelions and dances around on the top of the flower. They are so soft, and it is like being on a really thick carpet. After that, he finds the dandelion with the fluffs on the top. He flies past them as fast as he can, beating his wings, and trying to lift as much of the fluff as possible to see it flying through the air.

"Good afternoon, dandelions," Bert says as he flies past.

After he has had his fun, Bert flies off in search of crocuses. Crocuses are big, bold, bright flowers with lots of pollen. Crocus is a fun word to say too, and Bert likes to say it over and over in his head as he flies towards them.

" Good afternoon, crocuses, crocuses, crocuses," Bert says.

He does not have much room left by this point, so he collects as much as he can carry, and his pollen collecting is done for the day. But, there is still time to visit a few more flowers before he goes home.

"Good Afternoon, daisies," Bert says as he flies past them. He loves the large white petals and yellow center. It reminds him of the eggs that he once saw in a house he was trapped in. Thankfully the owner opened the window and let him out.

Good evening, hibiscus," Bert says as the sun starts to go back down. All the colors of the rainbow will soon be seen in the sky again, and that will mean that it is time for him to be in the hive. He likes the smell of hibiscus and knows that some humans make tea from it. Bert hopes that they add some of his honey to that tea.

"Good evening, magnolias," Bert says when he gets to the large white flowers. After seeing so much color throughout the day, it is nice to see a plain white flower, and Bert finds a lot of beauty there.

"Good evening, lotus," Bert says. This is his last stop of the evening. They have perfectly shaped petals, and they always seem to sway in the wind as he passes, like they are waving to him.

As Bert flies back to the hive, he is sad that he cannot visit more flowers. They are all so beautiful that he wishes he could stay out and visit more, but it is getting late, and he needs to deliver his pollen. Bert is getting tired, too, even with his morning nap.

When he gets home, he delivers his pollen and finds his bed. When he falls asleep, he dreams only of flowers. Bert cannot wait to wake up and visit the flowers again.

Uncle Ron Babysits

Hello.

My name is Albert, and I am a dinosaur. Most people call me Alby, and you can, too, if you want. You are reading this story about me, so you might as well.

I live in a house with my mom, dad, little sister Alison, and little brother Carlo. As you can imagine, we like to do the regular dinosaur things like roar, eat lots of food, and stomp around with our large feet.

I am a tyrannosaurus rex, so my favorite food is meat, though I try to eat lots of vegetables too. I have lots of sharp teeth, and I have to remember to brush them all before I go to bed, or they might fall out.

I am excited because my mom and dad are going out tonight. I am not excited about that part, they are pretty fun to have around, and they always play with me, but it does mean that Uncle Ron is coming to babysit us. Whenever my parents go out, he always comes to look after us, and he is the most fun uncle in the world.

He always calls us little troublemakers, which is funny because we cause almost no trouble at all.

When the knock came at the door, I ran downstairs to greet Uncle Ron. He always does the same knock: knock, knock, knock, then a long silence, then knockety-knock! I always get butterflies in my stomach when I hear that knock because I know that we are about to have lots of fun.

"Uncle Ron!" I shouted as I ran into his arms.

"Hello, troublemaker," said Uncle Ron. See what I said about him calling us troublemakers?

My little brother and little sister followed soon after.

"More troublemakers!" shouted Uncle Ron.

"You kids be good for Uncle Ron," said my dad as he put on his jacket.

"We will," the three of us said together.

"Call me if you need anything," said my mom as she put her hat on.

"We'll be fine," said Uncle Ron. He hugged my mom and closed the door behind her.

"Can we go and do something fun tomorrow?" I asked.

"Woah, I'm just in the door," said Uncle Ron.

"Can we go to the park to play, and have ice cream, and feed the ducks?" I asked.

"Feed the ducks!" shouted Alison. "Can we do that? Can we please. Can we go to the cinema too and get snacks?"

"And play in the arcade, and go to the library, and go for a hike," added Carlo.

"Woah, woah, woah," said Uncle Ron with his arms in the air. "That is a lot of things. Look, tomorrow, I am busy. How about we start tonight with some food? Who wants mac and cheese?"

"I do! I do! I do!" we all shouted together.

"Okay, you go and watch some TV, and I will whip up some dinner," said Uncle Ron.

The three of us went into the living room, and I was just about to switch on the TV when Carlo had a better idea. He suggested that instead of watching a TV show, we should paint a picture for Uncle Ron.

Alison suggested that we paint it on the wall so that it was really big. I thought that was a great idea, so we gathered all the paints that we had and painted a massive picture on the living room wall, with everything that we wanted to do with him. We finished just in time.

"Who wants mac and cheese?" announced Uncle Robert as he walked into the living room, carrying a giant pot of mac and cheese.

As soon as he saw the large painting on the wall, his mouth opened wide. He must have been so surprised at the amazing painting. Then, he dropped the mac and cheese, and it splashed all over the floor.

I tried to help clean it up while Alison and Carlo went off in search of our cleaning bucket.

I really did want to help, but I somehow managed to get the mac and cheese all over the sofa and the rest of the furniture in the room. When Alison and Carlo returned, they had somehow forgotten about the cleaning bucket, had gone out into the yard, and covered themselves in mud. There were now muddy footprints and handprints all over the house.

"Argh!" shouted Uncle Ron.

He's always really funny when he makes that noise. I think that he makes it just to make us laugh because he does it a lot.

"Into the bath!" shouted Uncle Ron. He scooped up Alison, Carlo, and me and took us up to the bathroom, the mac and cheese mixing with the mud as he did.

When we got there, he placed us all down and turned on the faucet. He added a little splash of bubble bath and went to get the towels.

"We need more," said Carlo. He squirted more into the bath.

"That's not how you do it," said Alison. She took the bottle, shook it, and added some more.

"You are doing it wrong," I said, taking the bottle. I added the rest of it to the bath.

When Uncle Ron came back, he could not find us with all the bubbles in the room. The three of us ran out of the bathroom to get some air and went downstairs. Uncle Ron followed us, but he must have forgotten to turn the bathwater off because water started cascading down the stairs like a waterfall.

"NO!" he shouted. "You three wait here while I turn the water off."

Well, we felt bad that Uncle Ron had made such a mess, so we decided to help him. We got the paint from the shed and started to repaint the living room. White was such a boring color, and lime green would look so much better.

When Uncle Ron came back downstairs, we had painted three rooms in lime green, including all of the furniture and the mac and cheese.

I don't think Uncle Ron liked it, but art is very subjective. He put his hands on his head and spun in a circle, looking at the newly-painted rooms.

"Argh!" he shouted again, and the three of us laughed. It was a very funny noise.

"Okay, okay, okay," he said. "We need to clean this up. Your parents are going to be home soon."

"They can clean it up," said Carlo. "They are very good at cleaning things up."

"It's true," said Alison.

I wanted to agree with them, but I didn't think that it would help. Instead, I said, "Okay, we'll help you clean up your mess, but you have to do all that fun stuff with us tomorrow."

"Anything," said Uncle Ron.

"Even feeding the ducks?" asked Alison.

"Yes!" said Uncle Ron.

"And the arcade?" asked Carlo.

"Yes, yes, yes, just clean!" he shouted.

We were about to start when we saw our parents pull up in their dinosaur car. We had fifteen seconds to get the house cleaned and repainted. The four of us worked together, cleaning as fast as we could. As my parents opened the door, we wiped the last surface. The house was as clean as it had ever been.

"Did you all have fun?" asked my father.

"Oh, yes," the three of us said.

"Did you all behave for Uncle Ron?" asked my mother.
"We did," the three of us said.

"Can I take them out tomorrow to do something fun?" asked Uncle Ron with a big frown on his face.

The there of us looked at him and smiled.

When Aliens Attack

Mark lay in his bed, and his mom read him a bedtime story. This was his favorite time of the day, and he loved most to hear stories about outer space. His mom would read him stories about space travel, amazing planets, and aliens from other planets.

As his mom read, Mark stared out of the window to the moon and stars above. He wondered if there really were aliens out there, and what they would look like. He reached his hand up to try to touch the stars and quickly recoiled it.

There was dried mud on his hands, and he had to hide them. He had spent most of the day playing in mud, throwing mud, and making delicious mud pies. If his mom saw his muddy hands, she would make him clean them, and clean hands are no fun.

He liked to let the wet mud dry on his hands until it started to crack. Then, he would pretend that he was an alien with weird mud hands.

"The end," said his mom.

Mark had forgotten all about the story and had been too busy imagining what aliens looked like. That didn't matter, he could always ask her to read the story again tomorrow night.

"Goodnight," said Mark.

"Goodnight," said his mom.

"I love you," said Mark.

"I love you too," said his mom. She turned off the light in his room and switched on the nightlight. It was a mini-moon that glowed.

Mark lay in his bed for a long time and eventually fell fast asleep. When he dreamed, he dreamed of aliens and faraway planets. As the sun woke him in the morning, he wiped his eyes with the back of his hands, but he could not get rid of the sleepy feeling.

When Mark opened his eyes, everything felt wrong.

This was not the light of the sun! It was much too bright, and coming from somewhere closer. Mark jumped out of bed and ran to the window, shielding his eyes. It looked like a giant spotlight coming from just above his house.

There was a noise too. It was a deep rumbling that shook the house around him. He had to cling onto the window frame so that he did not lose his balance. He shielded his eyes again and stared up at what was hovering above.

Mark could not believe it.

It was an alien spaceship!

Mark waved to it and tried to shout hello, but there was no response, and it was much too loud to hear anything over the deep rumbling. Suddenly, the noise changed, and more beams of light came from the spaceship. Mark could see that a few spaceships were hovering over the houses in his town.

Then it happened. All of the parents were lifted from their beds and transported up into the spaceships. Mark could hear the other children in his town calling, and he started to shout out too when his mom and dad started to float up to the spaceship.

When all the adults were taken, a funny melody was sounded, and all of the children fell fast asleep.

Mark jumped up when he woke. He could remember everything that had happened the night before. He ran outside and saw the spaceships. They were hovering close to the ground, but they were not doing anything else.

There were children outside too, looking up at the spaceships, and more were coming from houses, shaking themselves awake as they realized that all of the adults had been taken.

Some children think that it would be fun to have no parents around, but it is not much fun when your parents have been taken by aliens.

Mark quickly found his friends.

"Have your parents been taken too?" he asked.

"Yes," said Susan.

"Gone," said Will.

"What are we going to do?" asked Susan.

"I don't know," said Mark. He had the most knowledge of aliens, so the other two waited for him to think of a plan. "We have to attack them," he said finally.

The rallying cry went around, and all of the children grabbed weapons. Some found large rocks, others found tree branches, and a few had metal pipes. Mark had become their unofficial leader.

"Charge!" shouted Mark.

Those with tree branches ran towards the spaceships, getting as close as they could, but they were thrown back by a shield when they touched the ships. It glowed green as they touched it, and it stopped anything from getting through.

"Throw!" shouted Mark.

The rocks came next. Anyone who had a rock threw it at the closest spaceship. Mark watched the rocks arc through the air, and he crossed his fingers. But, when the rocks got within a few inches, the shield activated, and all of the rocks bounced harmlessly away without leaving so much as a dent.

"Final attack!" shouted Mark.

Those with metal pipes ran at the spaceships. This time, they did not get too close and tried to hit the spaceships from a few feet away. They struck down with the metal pipes and poles, hoping to do something but, before the pipes hit, the green shield activated. The pipes were thrown from the children's hands, and they were left standing there with no weapons.

Mark frowned. Not one spaceship had been damaged. The only thing that they had succeeded in doing was to dislodge some dirt that had been clinging to the bottom of the ships. If that was not bad enough, it started to rain.

The children found shelter under trees, and Mark watched the rain bouncing off the spaceships, and he wished that he had weapons made from rain.

"Hey," he said.

"What?" asked Susan.

"Look, the rain is hitting the spaceship and not the shield," said Mark.

"So it is," said Will. "But how does that help us? Are we going to spray water at the spaceships?"

"Not quite," said Mark. "Look at the bottom of the ships. There is some dirt there from when they have landed. Dirt can get through too."

"So, we throw dirt?" asked Susan.

"Almost," said Mark. "We combine the two. If we mix up some mud, we might be able to cover the spaceships in mud. That should do the job."

It was already raining, so it did not take much to turn the dirt into mud. The children formed a production line. Some added more water where needed, others mixed the dirt and water together, and the rest formed the mud into clumps that could be easily thrown.

Mark did the quality control, making sure that the mud was wet enough to stick, large enough to cover a lot of the ship, and light enough to be thrown.

When they had all of the mud weapons assembled, they went to work. The children picked up the mud clumps and threw them at the spaceships. There must have been at least ten thousand mud pies thrown that day.

They threw so much mud that the spaceships started to get heavy and fall slightly towards the ground. When all of the spaceships were completely covered, they heard a noise.

"Please, we surrender!"

Mark raised his hand to stop anyone from throwing any more mud. After a moment, the front of one spaceship opened, followed by the fronts of all the others. The parents walked down the ramps and ran to their kids. Everyone cheered.

As Mark hugged his parents, he looked up into the closest spaceship. There was a large green goo standing there. It did not have a face, but he was sure that it had a frown on its face. Mark waved to it as the door to the spaceship closed.

As quick as they had come, the aliens left Earth. From that day on, all the children of the world kept puddles of mud in their yards just in case the aliens should ever come back.

The Trapped Fairy

Winterbloom flapped her wings and lifted herself through the bright garden. The house lay at the edge of her forest, and whoever lived there took great care of the trees, bushes, and plants.

Winterbloom was a fairy, and she liked to fly through the bright petals and large green leaves in the garden, stopping at the small fish pond to wash her dazzling red wings. Of course, she would never let the human who lived there see her. She knew that there were good humans in the world, but she did not want to risk it. They might keep her as a pet, and that would not be a very good life.

No, she liked to fly free. She was a fairy, after all, and fairies are free beings. They do not want to live as pets, and they rarely live with other fairies. They live by themselves but get together with their friends a lot to have parties and each marigold cupcakes.

Winterbloom lopped in the air and landed on a small bush. Some bright blue berries were growing, and they would soon be ripe enough to pluck and eat. She watched the fish swimming below and wondered what it would be like to live in the water. The fish pond looked much too small for her, and she was glad that she had the entire forest to live in.

She picked one of the berries and ate it. It was a little sweet, but she would not pick any more, not just yet. She was about to turn around and fly back into the forest when she smelled the most delicious smell. It was a similar smell to the berry, but much sweeter.

A glance towards the house and she could see what was causing the aroma. On the kitchen windowsill, there was a pie, fresh from the oven. Whoever lived there must have baked it with the same berries from the garden.

Winterbloom hovered closer and found her mouth-watering. She thought about taking a bite from the pie or sampling just a little bit of it, but she might get caught doing it, and it was not hers to take. Instead, she sat on the windowsill for a while and smelled the delicious smell.

"Mmm, that smells so nice," said Winterbloom.

She was about to fly away when she caught sight of the inside of the house. She had looked through the window before, but she had never been so close to the inside. There were so many cool things to look at.

There were large seats with cushions on the top. She had a small chair in her tiny house, but it was nothing like this one. There was also a place in the wall to have a fire. Winterbloom jumped up and down.

"Whoever heard of having a fire inside your home," she whispered.

She was about to leave, even though there were so many fascinating things when she saw something that deserved a closer look.

"I really shouldn't go inside," whispered Winterbloom, "but I have to."

She had spotted a painting on the wall. In the painting, there were lots of daisies, and, below the daisies, fairies were dancing. The fairies did not look exactly like fairies look in real life, but they were pretty close. Winterbloom wondered if a human had seen a fairy before.

Before she knew what she was doing, she found herself flying into the house. She flew straight to the picture on the wall and examined all of the beautiful colors. In the picture, the fairies were all dancing, and Winterbloom felt like dancing too.

Swoosh!

Winterbloom turned around and froze. There was a woman who stood at the window with her back to her. The woman had closed the window and was lifting up the pie. As she turned around, Winterbloom flattened herself against the painting and made herself look like she was dancing.

The woman looked straight at the painting, shook her head as if she were imagining things, and walked away towards the kitchen.

Winterbloom let out a sigh of relief. She let her heartbeat slow and flew back over to the window. It was closed all the way. She tried to lift it up, but it was too heavy. She was stuck in the house. Winterbloom knew that she had to get out of there before she was spotted.

She could not hear the woman, so she looked around. There were no other windows in the room, and the only door was where the woman had gone.

"There is the fireplace!" whispered Winterbloom in delight. She flew over to it, perched herself on the logs, and looked up. It was completely black. She flew up a little way, but there was no way out, it was blocked entirely by soot.

Winterbloom sneezed, and a cloud of black soot flew up around her. When she came back out of the fireplace, she no longer had red wings. They were mostly black with specks of red. Most of her body was covered in black. She looked like a bat.

"Well, I guess that I have no other option," said Winterbloom.

There was only one thing to do, and that was to leave the living room and try to find a way out. She visited a few rooms but did not find anything useful.

One room had large books all over the walls, but there was no time to sit in there and read.

Another room had a large container that looked like it might be another pond, but there was a hole in the bottom. Water dripped from a metal pipe and ran down the hole. There was a smaller container that almost looked like a seat. There was a small amount of water in the bottom of it, and Winterbloom drank some of it. She was very thirsty.

The next room had lots of food in it, but some was in a very cold box, and Winterbloom almost got herself trapped in there. She would not have minded that for there were many delicious cakes and other sweet treats in there.

She would have stayed in there is she had not heard the scream.

"Aargh!!!! A bat!" screamed the woman.

"I'm a fairy," said Winterbloom indignantly, though the woman did not understand what she said. Humans cannot speak the fairy language.

Winterbloom had only just looked up when a broom came crashing down towards her head. She flapped her wings and took to the air. The woman screamed some more, and blindly swung the broom around her head in large circles.

Winterbloom flew from room to room, but there were no open windows or doors. She wondered why the woman was so angry. Had she never seen a fairy before? Winterbloom flew back to the window and tried to open it, but she could not. There were tiny fairy footprints and handprints all across the house.

When all seemed lost, the woman threw open the front door and shouted, "Shoo!"

Winterbloom had heard that word before, and thought that is must have meant something like, "I have opened the door for you, you are welcome to leave."

So, she did. Winterbloom flew past the woman, waved at her as she did, and flew from the house. When she was outside, she gave a little laugh. It had been a fun adventure, especially with how ridiculous the woman had looked swinging the broom around her head.

From that day forth, Winterblloom never went into another house ever again, no matter how nice it smelled.

The Boy With No Birthday

Once, there was a boy who had no birthday. No one knew how old he was, and no matter how much he searched, he could not find his birthday.

"Mom, when is my birthday?" asked the boy.

"I don't remember," said his mom. "I think that it might be sometime in November."

"Dad, do you know when my birthday is?" asked the boy.

"Hmm," replied his dad. "I think that it might be on a Wednesday."

"Grandma, when was I born?" asked the boy.

"I think that it might have been in 2012," said his grandma with a hoarse whisper.

"Grandpa, you must know when my Birthday is," said the boy, a little exasperated at not being able to find his birthday.

"The moon!" shouted his grandpa. That really did not help.

So, the boy was left to look for his birthday on his own. He could not remember being born, that would be ridiculous. He tried to remember as far back as he could, but he could not remember anything from his youth. It had been a long time since his youth, almost two years, and he could not remember that far back.

He might remember a birthday party, but he was not sure if it was his. He would have to do some more detective work.

The boy went to his closet. He remembered getting some presents, but that could have been from Christmas, it was hard to tell. He searched through his closet and found some toys that he had received recently, but there were no clues there.

He got a little distracted and decided to play with his toys for a little while. He built with his blocks, building a large tower. After that, he lined up his toy soldiers and knocked them over with his Nerf gun. Then, he tried to stack all of his soft toys as big as he could, and he followed that up by building a large fort.

It was only when he found a piece of wrapping paper that he remembered about his mission. He was supposed to be looking for his birthday, and he had forgotten all about it. No wonder he had forgotten his birthday if this was how easily he got distracted.

"Hmm," said the boy, flipping the paper over and over in his hands. He could see the letter 'b 'on it, and there were no Christmas images, only a star, and a soccer ball. "I'm sure that this is from my birthday, so that proves that I do have a birthday. I just need to find out when it is."

The boy was tempted to play some more in his fort, but he had more important things to do. He walked downstairs and put on his jacket and hat.

"I'm going out," he said. "I'll be back soon." He had some people to visit.

First, he went to his other grandparents, who lived down the street. They were very sensible people and would surely know when his birthday was. If he only knew, he could discover how old he was, and begin to plan for his next birthday.

The boy knocked on the door, and his grandmother answered.

"Come in, come in," she said.

"Grandma, do you know when my birthday is?" asked the boy when he was inside.

"I think that I do," replied the grandma. "You know, that reminds me of the time when I went to Berlin. I was there for a work conference, very boring, it was all about elephants and how they can dance. Anyway, I was walking down the street when I bumped into an old friend of mine. She told me a story about the time she went boating in the Atlantic ocean and ran into pirates, very boring stuff. Still, it reminded her of the time that she had to answer the telephone, and that part is very interesting. You should pay attention now because it is all about school work."

The boy's grandma could really talk, and she often said a lot without saying anything at all. So, the boy let her talk while he asked his grandpa if he knew when his birthday was.

"Do you know when my birthday is, Grandpa?" asked the boy.

"Have you checked up your nose?" asked his grandpa.

The boy had not checked up his nose, but he was sure that it was not up there. How could it be? Well, he had come here to get some sensible answers, but it would seem that adults could be very silly when they wanted to be.

"I have to go," said the boy.

"But you have not even had any cakes yet," said his grandma.

"Well, maybe I could stay for that," said the boy. There were some things in life that were a little more important than finding out when your birthday was, and cake was one of those things.

When the boy had a stomach full of cakes, he went off in search of his friends. If anyone was going to remember when his birthday was, they surely would.

Karen was already playing on the street. She was whizzing up and down on her scooter.

"Karen, do you know when my birthday is?" asked the boy.
"Your birthday?" asked Karen, a little surprised. "No, I have no idea. Oh, look at the time. I have to go." She whizzed away.

The boy knocked on Lucas's door next.

"Lucas, when is my birthday?" asked the boy.

"Is this a trick question?" asked Lucas. He closed the door, and the boy was left standing there alone.

There was one friend left to try, his best friend. If anyone was going to know, it would be Lily.

"Lily," said the boy when he finally caught up to her. She was running down the street. "When is my birthday?"

"No time, got to go," said Lily. She ran away as fast as she could.

The boy did not know what to do. He had lost his birthday, and he did not think that he would ever find it. He had nothing else to do but go home.

"Maybe I will stay the same age forever," said the boy.

When he got home, he was feeling sad, and he hung his head down and put on a frown to make himself look extra sad. He opened the door and walked into his house.

"Surprise!" shouted everyone.

The boy looked up with a big smile on his face. He had found his birthday. His parents were there. All his grandparents were there. All of his friends were there. He was not sure how he had done it, but he had found it.

This time, he was not going to lose it again. He looked at the calendar. January 7th. He opened his personal notebook and grabbed a pen to write the date down. On the first page, in big, bold letters, was the words:

January 7th: BIRTHDAY!

The words were underlined six times. He underlined them one more time.

"That should help me to remember," whispered the boy.

He put the book back in his pocket and enjoyed the birthday party, There were lots of presents, and he tore the wrapping off of them excitedly. His grandma had brought lots of cake with her, and he found room to put more cakes in his belly. There were even fun games and dancing. When the party was done, the boy was happier than he had ever been.

His friends said goodbye, and everyone left. The boy sat on the couch with a belly full of cake.

"Now," he said to himself. "I just need to find out what my name is."

The Baby That Could Not Sleep

There once was a baby that could not sleep. No matter what anyone did, the baby would not sleep. When it was time for bed, the baby would be put into its crib, and then it would start to cry. It would cry and cry and cry.

"Waaaaaaaaaaaaaaaaaaaaaaaaaa!" shouted the baby as it lay down in its crib.

"Oh, no," said his mother. "We need to do something." She quickly ran around the house with her hands on her head, humming an exasperated tune. She was sure that she had all of her baby books only a few minutes ago, and now they all seemed to be missing. She looked under the couch cushions, in the bathtub, and she even searched through the freezer. She hung her head in shame when she could not find them.

When she got back to the baby room, she remembered that she had left them beside the baby crib. She let out a little laugh and picked up the first book. The baby cried even louder.

"Waaaaaaaaaaaaaaaaaaaaaaaaaa!" shouted the baby.

His mother opened the first book and read it as quickly as she could. When she was done reading the book, the baby was crying even louder. So, she opened another book. This one was about a nice dragon and really was a wonderful story. But, when she was done, the baby was only crying more. So, she tried a third. This book was about trees that dance, and the mother was sure that it would help her baby. When she was done, the baby was crying more.

"Waaaaaaaaaaaaaaaaaaaaaaaaaa!" screamed the baby.

"I don't know what to do," said the mother.

"I think that I know what needs to be done," said the baby's father. "He is just not calm enough to sleep. I am going to give him a bath."

The father ran off and put some water in the bath. He added cold water first, then some hot, then some cold to make it cool again. He needed to add some hot water after that because he had made it too cold again. Then it was too hot, then too cold, then too hot, then too cold, then too hot, then it was just right.

He ran back to the bedroom and picked up the crying baby. He unwrapped the blanket, took off the baby onesie, pulled off the tiny socks, removed the diaper (thankfully it was empty), and placed the baby gently in the bath.

"Coo, coo, coo, coo," sang his father.

He scooped up some water and ran it over the baby's head. He added some shampoo and washed the hair before rinsing it. He washed between the baby's toes and in the crooks of his elbows. He even washed the baby's bum. When the baby was as clean as a baby can get, his father removed him from the water.

He dried the baby from head to toe, even getting into the spaces between the toes. He put some powder on the baby and put on a fresh diaper (it would not stay fresh for long). He put the tiny socks back on and the baby onesie. He wrapped the blanket around the baby, and placed the baby back in the crib, placing a hundred stuffed toys around his baby boy.

The baby cried louder.

"Waaaaaaaaaaaaaaaaaaaaaaaaaa!" cried the baby.

"No, no," said the baby's oldest sister. "He is unhappy because he wants to play. Once he had played, he will go to sleep."

She picked up one of the toys and danced it in front of the baby's face. The teddy bear danced from side to side as the baby cried.

A stuffed penguin was chosen next. The penguin hopped up and down on the baby's belly. The oldest sister made it sing as it danced around the crib.

Next up were a lion and a tiger dancing together. The oldest sister gave them voices and made them sing to each other as they danced around the crib.

The oldest sister juggled three of the stuffed bird toys next, but that did not help to calm the baby. He only cried louder.

"Waaaaaaaaaaaaaaaaaaaaaaaaaa!" he cried louder than before.

The oldest sister tried to make the animals talk to her baby brother. She made the animals tell him that he was safe now and that it was time to sleep, and they would be there to protect him. But, no matter what she did, her baby brother cried. And, it seemed that the more that she tried to calm him, the louder her cried.

"Waaaaaaaaaaaaaaaaaaaaaaaaa!" cried the baby, even louder than he had before.

"I know what to do," said the baby's older brother. He was only five years old, but he already had lots of great ideas. "He needs some human interaction."

His parents had no idea where he had heard the words *human interaction*, but there were willing to try anything. They watched as the older brother picked up the baby and held him to his shoulder. He slowly bounced the baby up and down on his shoulder.

"Waaaaaaaaaaaaaaaaaaaaaaaaa!" cried the baby.

He sang a sweet song into his ear, moving slowly around the room, being the best big brother in the world. His older sister watched. His parents watched. The baby even seemed to watch before he started to cry again.

"Waaaaaaaaaaaaaaaaaaaaaaaaaa!" screamed the baby. If it were possible, the baby was crying even louder than before, and it was crying pretty loudly before. Everyone in the room wondered how something so small could make so much noise.

"Waaaaaaaaaaaaaaaaaaaaaaaaaa!" the baby cried again.

The older brother patted his baby brother on the back and told him that it was going to be okay. He put his face in front of his baby brother's face and made reassuring noises. He tried pulling funny faces to make his brother laugh, but that did not work. No matter what he did, no matter what anyone did, the baby only continued to cry.

"Waaaaaaaaaaaaaaaaaaaaaaaaaa!" the baby cried.

"There is only one thing that we can do," said the father. "We have to work together. We should all sing a lullaby together, and that will surely calm him. If we do that, we will surely soothe him."

"What about Lavender?" asked the older brother. Lavender was the youngest girl in the house, but she was already fast asleep. She was two years old, and a very good sleeper. Her baby brother had not followed in her footsteps.

"It will just have to be the four of us," said the father.

So, the four of them agreed on which song to sing, and they began to sing it. The song is a beautiful song, but they did not sing it beautifully. They were awful singers, and they were even worse when they sang together. It was the worst thing that had ever been heard in the history of the world.

You can guess what happened next. Yes, the baby began to cry even louder.

"Waaaaaaaaaaaaaaaaaaaaaaaaaa!" cried the baby as loud as it could.

"What are you all doing?" asked Lavender. She was stood in the doorway of the baby room with a sleepy expression on her face.

"We are trying to calm your baby brother," said her mother. "He won't stop crying."

"Waaaaaaaaaaaaaaaaaaaaaaaaaa!" cried the baby.

"Well, no wonder," said Lavender. "I would be the same if I had so many people fussing over me. You should leave him alone to sleep."

"Leave him alone," said her mother.

"Huh," said her father.

"That's an idea," said her older brother.

"Maybe we could try it," said her older sister.

So, the four of them left the room, and, three minutes later, there was no sound from the room. The baby had fallen fast asleep.

The Weird Guy

Bill was a very weird guy.

He did not like to sleep in a bed like most regular people do. He does not have a comfortable mattress like you and me, nor does he have a nice soft pillow to rest his head on. You might think that he has a warm blanket to curl up under when it gets cold, but you would be wrong.

Bill has a solid wooden board that he sleeps on. He likes to have a solid wooden board because it is good for his back. It helps to keep his back straight when he is sleeping, and that makes him happy. Of course, if he flips onto his stomach, then his belly becomes straight instead, but he does not mind this.

In place of a pillow, Bill paces his head on a cat. Cats are very soft, and this cat will wake Bill in the morning, so he does not need an alarm clock. The cat likes Bill, so he tolerates having a large head on him.

While most people like to have a blanket or comforter to keep themselves warm during the night, Bill uses a sleeping bag. He found that blankets are so often knocked off the bed during the night, so he zips himself up inside a sleeping bag so that only his eyes are showing. Bill is never cold during the night, and this makes him happy.

When morning comes, and the cat meows, Bill knows that it is time to get up. It is much better to be woken by a friendly cat that it is to be woken by a loud alarm clock, and you do not have to turn off a cat, so this saves Bill three seconds every morning. Bill likes to save time. It makes him happy.

Bill heard a scientist talking on the radio one afternoon, and the scientist claimed that it is better to brush your teeth with charcoal than with toothpaste, so that is exactly what Bill does every morning. He does not use toothpaste to brush his teeth, he uses charcoal. His teeth might be black by the time he is done, but he has never had any cavities, and this makes Bill happy.

Bill has always wondered why there is breakfast food. You can eat lunch food for dinner, and dinner food for lunch, but why is breakfast food eaten at breakfast. I mean, you can eat breakfast food for dinner and snacks, but you wouldn't eat dinner for breakfast. *You* wouldn't, but Bill would.

Bill had never really been one for cereal and toast. He liked them occasionally but did not want to have them every morning. He much preferred roast dinners. For breakfast this morning, he cooked himself up a roast chicken, Brussels sprouts, roast potatoes, corn, and gravy. When he was done, he had pumpkin pie for breakfast dessert. This made Bill happy.

When you work in an office, you usually wear a suit. Can you guess who does not wear a suit when he works in an office? Bill did wear a suit for the first couple of days but soon grew tired of it. When he turned up to work in shorts and a t-shirt, he got some funny stares.

He was even called into his boss's office and given a good talking to. A good talking to is never usually very good and is usually bad, which is weird. Maybe there are more weird people in this world than just Bill.

Anyway, Bill's boss could not help but agree that Bill still did his work, no matter what he was wearing. In fact, it was probably true that Bill did more work when he was wearing his shorts and t-shirt. He was not restricted by a tie or tight pants, or a stuffy shirt or jacket. When he was freed of that unnecessary clothing, he could work harder and smarter.

There was some talk of everyone wearing shorts and t-shirts to work, and this made Bill happy.

I should also tell you about how Bill says hello and goodbye.

Bill does not say hello, he says, "Howdy-diddly-doody."

Bill does not say goodbye, he says, "See ya later, Tater."

This gets him some funny looks when he says it, and people think that he is extra weird. Yet, once they walk away, they cannot help but feel a smile come to their faces. If Bill knew how much his words made people happy, he would be even happier.

When it is your birthday, anniversary, or some other special occasion, you probably won't get a present from Bill. He likes to give presents at random times of the year, and he gives presents because he likes people or they have done something special.

You won't get a present on Christmas, but you might get one on June 9th. You also won't get a present because it has been a certain number of years since you were born, but you might get one if you work hard to help people who have a hard life. People always expect presents at certain times of the year, but it is much more fun to get a present when you are not expecting it.

On his lunch break, Bill likes to go for a run. But, he does not run like everyone else. He does not want to waste time running for a long time, so he runs as fast as he can for as long as he can. When he cannot run anymore, he walks back to the office and has his lunch.

Sometimes, for lunch, he will have a big slice of cake and some ice cream. Sometimes he will have asparagus dipped in ketchup. Occasionally, he will have a slice of lamb with peanut butter on it. He will eat whatever he wants to eat. He thinks people who eat things that they don't want to eat are weird.

Bill also has a pet, thought the bird does not know that it is a pet. When the bird visited his yard one day to eat some seed, Bill took a liking to it. He had always thought it weird that people buy animals and then keep them in their houses—no wonder those animals spend so much time trying to get out.

Bill named the bird Tweeter. It visits his yard every day, and Bill holds out his hand full of seed for the bird to land on and eat. Sometimes other birds come too, and that is fine because they are friends of his pet bird. Tweeter is the best pet that he has ever owned. I should mention that the cat he uses as a pillow is not his pet. It wandered into his house one day and never left.

Before bed, Bill likes to fill a basin with jello and stick his feet into it. Why does he do this? Because it feels good. It also makes his feet smell like lemon or strawberry or peaches. The cat seems to like it too and will lick his feet clean. It tickles and makes him laugh.

At bedtime, Bill will read himself a bedtime story. There is no one else around to do it, so he has to do it himself. He always chooses a good story and reads it well, doing all of the voices. While he reads, he has grapes and milk. He likes to dip the grapes into the milk.

When he gets into bed, he stretches five times before zipping up his sleeping bag. As he falls asleep, he always smiles.

Some people might think that he is weird, but Bill is almost certainly the happiest person in the world.

How To Calm Your Mind

Sometimes it can be hard to relax.

There are times when you get into bed, and you just cannot switch off your mind. You might have had something exciting happen during the day, and you cannot stop thinking about it, or you might have something that is worrying you, and you cannot get it out of your head.

It can be hard to have worries, and it can be very hard to stop thinking about them. There are times when, no matter what you do, you cannot get rid of the worries from your mind.

Even if you have something fun and exciting in your mind, it can cause you trouble if you cannot sleep.

When we go to sleep, it gives our minds some time to rest, and that is very important for everyone. When you cannot sleep, your mind cannot rest, and then all of your problems can get worse.

When you sleep, your brain has time to process all of the information that it has collected over the day, and you usually collect a lot of information. It is also a time when your brain deals with problems.

Have you ever had a problem that you could not solve or a problem that was causing you a lot of trouble, and felt sad about it? Have you ever gone to sleep and felt better about it in the morning? That is because your brain can help to solve your problems when you are sleeping.

It doesn't even matter if you solve the problem or not, after sleeping, you usually feel better about any problems that you may have. Sleep is a wonderful thing, and it is very important.

So, when it is hard to sleep, not only does your body feel more tired, your brain does too. If you cannot sleep well, your problems are going to seem worse than they are, and you are never going to solve them.

This story is here to help you to switch off your brain and get to sleep. When that happens, all of your problems are going to diminish. This means that they are not going to be as bad as they first seem. They might still be problems, but big problems will shrink into small problems, and small problems will pop like balloons.

Balloons are important for this, so get ready to think about lots of different balloons.

Everyone has problems, so we are going to start with your problems and get them out of the way so that you can sleep. The best part is that you do not have to talk about your problems if you do not want to, but it is always better to share a problem is you can. When you share a problem, it cuts it in half immediately, and the person who you tell it to can often help.

Okay, back to clearing your mind.

Make sure that you are comfortable in your bed and close your eyes.

If you need to get any wiggles out of the way, do it now. Shake your body, wriggle your toes and fingers, get all of that energy out of your body, and relax.

With your eyes closed, you are going to think of a big problem. What big problem did you encounter today? It can be anything that you want. If it is a big problem for you, then it is a big problem, and do not let anyone tell you otherwise.

Now, think about that big problem and how it makes you feel. It probably doesn't feel good, does it? That is okay, problems do not make anyone feel good.

Now, imagine this problem in your mind. It might take the form of the problem. Maybe your problem is about sharing, and you can imagine not sharing or having someone not share with you. Think about a specific incident if you can.

If there is not a specific incident, then think of how you feel. Maybe you are sad, but don't know why. What does that sadness look like? Does it look like a big blue cloud, a scary snake, something else?

Think of an image that represents your problem. Now, add all the emotion to that image, and hold it in your mind.

Get ready to scream!

We are not going to scream out loud, we are going to scream in our minds. In your mind, take a balloon. It is not blown up yet, but it soon will be. Put the ballon to your mouth and, in your mind, scream into it. Scream about your big problem, filling up the balloon. As you scream in your mind, the balloon will get bigger and bigger, but it does not burst.

When you have screamed all of your problem, let go of the balloon. It will magically tie itself in front of you. Your problem is still there, but it is now inside the balloon. Imagine the balloon in your mind. How big is it? What shape is it? What color is it?

The balloon floats in front of you, and it is now time to send it deep into your mind so that your brain can work on it while you sleep.

As you keep your eyes closed, you find that you have a massive pin in your hand. It is very sharp at one end, and the point glistens in the light. When you are ready, bring up the pin and stab it into the balloon. As you do, the balloon burst with a big 'POP! 'and the problem disappears from your mind.

Good job, you are helping yourself to become a better person.

Now, we are going to do the same with your next big problem. Think about it in your mind, imagine what it looks like, scream it into a balloon, and pop that balloon when you are ready. Do this for as many big problems as you have.

After this, you can concentrate on the smaller problems. Are there any things that have made you frustrated, angry, or sad, but you shouldn't really be annoyed by them? Maybe you didn't get ice cream after dinner, or someone stepped on your toe, or the sun wasn't shining today. It doesn't matter what it is, if it is a problem for you, then it is a valid problem.

Now, we are going to take all of those small problems and scream them into the same balloon, in your mind, of course.

Think about all of the problems together. Imagine as many of them as you can, think about how you feel, imagine shapes, colors, and anything else that comes to mind. When you have them all there, scream them all into a big balloon. This is going to be the biggest balloon ever. Keep screaming (in your mind) until you have filled the balloon with all of your problems.

How does it feel to have this giant balloon in front of you? What size is it? What shape is it? What color is it?

Are you ready to pop it?

Tale the large needle in your hand, and stick it into the balloon. Can you hear the large 'POP! 'as you burst it. Feels good, doesn't it? Let the problems be sent to the back of your mind so that your brain can deal with them while you sleep.

Your problems are still there, but you do not need to worry about them for a while, your brain will do that while you sleep.

Before you open your eyes, let go of the pin. When you do, it turns into birds. The birds fly away into the distance until you cannot see them anymore. When they are gone, your mind is blank, a safe space for you to be.

If you want to go to sleep, go to sleep now. If you are not ready, slowly open your eyes, and continue to relax.

Goodnight.

The Musical Animals

Lynne was a fox. The one thing that she loved to do more than anything in the world was to play her guitar. She would play it when she got up in the morning, and she would play it before she went to bed. She would also play it all of the time between getting up and going to bed.

She had been playing for as long as she could remember, and had gotten really good. She had practiced every day to become as good as she was, and continued to practice every day so that she got even better.

When you are good at something, you always need to keep practicing at it.

So, this is exactly what he did. Lynne practiced playing lots of different songs every day, and she was happy that she could play the guitar so well.

"But, I think that I could be better," said Lynne. "Yet, I don't know how."

"You already play so well," said her friend Roxy. "You could learn to play new songs."

"I have learned lots of new songs, but I think that something else is missing," said Lynne.

"What if you played a different instrument?" asked Roxy.

"No," said Lynne. "I like the guitar so much," said Lynne.

" Then, I don't know what," said Roxy.

"Me neither," said Lynne. "I'm going to go for a walk.

When Lynne went for a walk, she took her guitar with her. She always took her guitar everywhere. As she walked, she sang her favorite songs, creating a merry melody in the forest. As she wandered, she thought about what was missing from her playing. She was not sure that she could get any better on the guitar.

Bang! Bang! Dunk! Thunk! Boom, boom, boom! Krsh! Badoom!

Lynne liked the beat immediately. Someone was playing the drums. As Lynne listened, the drumbeat moved from fast to slow and back to fast again. At first, it seemed like there was no pattern to it, but Lynne soon found the pattern, and she started to play along.

As she got closer, she played louder, and the two instruments started to work in harmony. When Lynne was really close, the drumbeat stopped. Lynne stopped too.

A Squirrel popped its head out from the trunk of a tree.

"Oh, it's you," said Sandy, the squirrel.

"It's me," said Lynne.
"I have no idea who you are, but I like your guitar playing," said Sandy. "Do you want to play some more together?"

"Yes, please," said Lynne. "You are so good at playing the drums."

"I know," replied Sandy.

The two of them played together for hours, and Lynne found a little of what was missing from her life. She loved to play by herself, but playing with someone else made her own playing even better.

Sandy played the drums, and Lynne joined in with her own song. Then they swapped. Lynne started the beat, and Sandy joined in. They were amazing together.

"Hello?" A voice stopped them playing. Lynne and Sandy looked up to see a bear with a banjo.

"Can I play too?" asked Roland, the bear.

"Are you any good?" asked Sandy. "You have to be good to play with us."

"I don't know," said Roland.

"Of course you can play," said Lynne. "Don't listen to Sandy."

Roland walked over and stood beside Lynne. He held his banjo but did not say anything. Sandy did not waste any time and started banging on his drums. Lynne soon joined in, but Roland was a little more shy. It was not until Lynne smiled at him and nodded that he started to play.

Lynne was glad that he had turned up. As soon as Roland started playing his banjo, his fingers were a blur. He played so fast that Sandy could almost not keep up on the drums.

"This boy can play!" shouted Sandy when they had played their first song together.

As they played together, Sandy found a little more of what she was looking for. She realized that she needed people to share her music with. This was what would bring her joy. So, she put up adverts all around the forest.

It did not take long for lots more animals to join them in their jam sessions.

A snake came along with an accordion. There were three mice with trumpets. A wolf played the oboe. Two crocodiles played bass guitar. An owl sang lead vocals. Nine beavers sang backup vocals. A spider played the tuba. A bumblebee had a flute. The elephant was the last to join, he played the triangle.

When Lynne turned up to the jam session, she was excited to see so many animals with instruments.

"This is not going to work," said Sandy.

"It will work, just have a little faith," said Lynne.

Sandy beat the snare drum, starting a count, and all the animals joined in at the same time. Lynne almost stopped playing. She could see Roland smiling beside her, and he was just amazed as she was. They had never played all together before, yet they played with each other perfectly.

As Lynne smiled at Roland, she found some more of what she was looking for. She had been playing alone for so long, but she had so many musical friends now. Yet, there was still something missing. She was not sure, though, if they could fit in any more musicians.

When Lynne went home that night, she was happier than she had ever been, but she was still frustrated. She had found everything that she had been looking for, people to share her music with, but she still felt that something was missing.

"Why am I still unhappy when I am so happy?" Lynne whispered as she fell asleep that night.

The next day, she went back to the agreed practice spot and found most of the animals there. Roland was directing them. They were placing logs and branches on the ground, moving rocks, and flattering some grass.

"What is going on?" asked Lynne.

"You are not fully happy," said Roland.

"I am happy," claimed Lynne.

"No, I could see it in your smile yesterday," said Roland. "You are happy, but not fully happy, and I know why."

"Why?" asked Lynne. "She hoped that he had the answers that she was struggling to find.

"You want to share your music, right?" asked Roland.

"Yes, and I can do that with all of you," replied Lynne.

"But it is not enough," said Roland. "It is not enough for any of us. We want to share our music too, and not just with other musicians. We want to share it with everyone. That is why I put up all of these posters last night, with Sandy's help, of course."

Sandy was sitting in a tree branch and smiling.

Lynne looked at the poster. It was advertising a concert that was scheduled to happen in twenty minutes. It did not take long for all of the animals in the forest to turn up and take their seats.

Before Lynne could question what was happening, Sandy counted them in, and all of the animals started playing and singing. Lynne was caught up in it, and could not stop herself from playing.

The concert lasted for four hours, and the audience went crazy at the end, demanding an encore. Lynne and her band played for another hour. When they were done, everyone asked when the next concert would be. Lynne promised that it would be soon.

With the help of Sandy and Roland, Lynne had found everything that she had ever dreamed of.

The Oil Fountain

In the land of the robots, life was hard. Not that it was purposely hard, it just happened to be hard.

Robots are made out of metal, and that can make things difficult.

If you are made from skin and bones, like you and I are, some things are easy. Wait, I should not presume things. You are made from skin and bones, aren't you? Anyway, going out in the rain is no problem for the likes of us, not so for robots.

Because robots are made from metal, they cannot go out in the rain, or they might rust. They can, however, step on a nail and not have it hurt them. You do not want to step on a nail, believe me, it is not pleasant.

Rick was only two years old when he wanted to go and play in the rain.

"Go out! Go out! Go out!" he chanted.

"No, no, no," said his mother. "You cannot go out in this rain, or you will rust. That happened to your aunt Jane. She got caught in the rain, and she still cannot move her left leg."

When Rick was four, he started to ask more questions.

"Why can't we go out in the rain? It rains so much. Why does it rain so much, and why can't we go out in the rain?" asked Rick.

"If we get caught in the rain," said his mother, "we will start to rust. When that happens, it makes it hard for us to move, and there is no cure for that, just ask your Aunt Jane. As for why it rains so much, that I do not know. Now, go and play and stop worrying."

When he was six, he still could not understand why it rained so much.

"Why do we live in a world where rain makes us rust?" he asked.

No one had an answer for that.

When he was eight, he tried asking more questions.

"There surely must be a way to stop us from rusting, shouldn't there?" asked Rick.

"Not that I know of," replied his mother.

"There is the fountain of youth," spat his grandmother, an old clanky robot that sat in a metal rocking chair in the corner.

"Oh, mother," said Rick's mom. "Not this again."

"What is the fountain of youth?" asked Rick.

"It was a legend that my grandmother told me when I was a little girl. Somewhere there is a fountain that will keep you young," said his grandmother.

"It would have been found by now," said Rick's mom.

"It's in the Rainy Plains," said his grandmother.

"Where?" asked Rick.

"A place that you must never go," said Rick's mother.

"Your mother is right," said his grandmother. "It is a very dangerous place. It is a place where it rains almost all of the time. It is said that the fountain of youth is there."

"Why would it be in such a dangerous place?" asked Rick.

"Anything worth anything is usually hard to get," said his grandmother.

"But, why?" asked Rick.

"I don't know," said his grandmother. "That's just the way that things are sometimes."

"I would go," said Aunt Jane. She was stood in the corner looking out the window. "If I could." Ever since she had been caught in the rain a second time, both of her legs had seized up, and she could not sit down anymore.
When Rick turned nine, he had finally had enough. His Aunt Jane had been caught in the rain two more times, and she could only move her head now. Rick was not sure how she continued to smile. Maybe her lips had been rusted into a permanent smile.

Rick packed his adventure bag and headed for the Rainy Plains. When he got there, he stopped dead. There was rain falling, and he did not dare to get any closer. He pulled a nuts&bolts bar from his bag and chomped down on it.

He pulled his flashlight from his bag and pointed it at the Rainy Plains. That did nothing to help him. He pulled out a pen and paper. The Rainy Plains looked extensive, and there was a lot of rain. He had to be careful. He would do his best to map out the entire place.

When the rain finally stopped, he readied himself. He was about to run into the Rainy Plains when it started to rain again. He stopped running just in time and did not get wet.

When the rain stopped for a second time, he waited for a minute. When he started running, the rain started again, and he had to turn back.

He vowed to go for it as soon as the rain stopped.

When it stopped a third time, he took off running, moving between the trees that lined the Rainy Plains. He tried to map the area as much as he could. When there was an eruption of thunder, he quickly turned back. He had only just made it back out when the rain started again.
"A good start," he said. He had started his map, and he would be able to make it farther the next time.

When the next time came, he ran as fast as he could, drawing his map and looking for shelter. He spotted a rocky overhang in the distance but had already spent too much time in there. He turned back and ran out. The rain started soon after.

It rained for a long time and, when it stopped, Rick ran as fast as he could. He only just made it to the rocky overhang when the rain splashed down. Two seconds more and he would have been caught.

"No turning back," said Rick. He did not know if the fountain of youth was a real fountain, nor what it would be like, but he did know that if he got caught in the rain, he would never leave this place, and no one would come to rescue him.

When the rain stopped, he continued the adventure, this time from the rocky overhang. He darted back and forth, mapping out the area, and hoping to get closer to the fountain. When he found a cave, that became his new stopping point.

This time, his flashlight was useful. As he shone it into the dark cave, he saw some writing on the wall.

When you leave this cave, do not turn tail.
Keep moving, and you will prevail.
Move towards the mountain.
There you will find the fountain.

Rick knew what he had to do. He did not know how he knew, but he had the feeling that the fountain would save him from the rain. He had to believe that the words were meant for him.

"It's now or never," he said.

The rain stopped.

Rick ran.

He ran as fast as he could. He ran directly towards the mountain. After fifteen seconds, his mind told him to go back, but his heart kept his legs moving. He ran up the hill, and the rain started.

There it was!

In the distance, a fountain spurting black liquid into the air. The rain fell on him, but he could not stop. He could feel his arms seizing up. They hung unmoving at his sides as he continued to run.

His legs began to feel it. They were seizing up too. He was so close that he could smell it. It was the most wonderful aroma in the world. He was so close when his left leg seized up. He hopped as fast as he could, almost able to touch it. With his last ounce of strength, as his entire body seized up, he hopped one last hop and fell into the fountain.

It took a second, but the fountain of oil slowly lubricated all of his joints. It was still raining, but, after a few seconds, he could move freely.

Rick scooped up as much as he could in an empty container and walked out of the Rainy Plains. Everyone was amazed to see him. He went to his Aunt Jane first and lubricated her joints.

From that day forward, everyone visited the oil fountain, and no robot ever feared the rain again.

The Most Beautiful Flower In The World

"Remind me again?" asked Jessica. "Where are we going?"

"We are on an adventure," said her father.

"Yes, I know that," said Jessica. "But why are we on this adventure?"

"We are hunting for the most beautiful flower in the world," said her father.

"And, we cannot see it at home?" asked Jessica,

"No!" stated her father, astonished that she would even think such a thing. "There is only one place that the flower grows, and it only blooms once every hundred years. No one in our lifetime has ever seen it."

"Sounds pretty cool," said Jessica.

"It is cool," stammered her father. "It is cool. It will be cool. I hope that it is cool." He whispered the last part.

Jessica left him to his thoughts. She had been traveling for four days with her family, and there were still a number of days to go. She hoped that the flower would be worth it. From what she had been told, there was only one place where the flower bloomed, and, if they were too late, they would miss it entirely. Jessica was not sure that she could wait another hundred years to see it or if she would be alive in another hundred years.

She clung into the back of her camel as they rode through the desert. The first day in the desert had been tough going, but she was tolerating it more. There was sand as far as the eye could see, and it was hot. Really hot.

She pulled her scarf up over her head as the sun rose to its highest point. It would not protect from the rays of the sun, but it did protect her skin from burning.

"What do you think the flower is going to be like?" she asked her mother.

"I think that it is going to be the most colorful flower in the world," replied her mother. "I think that it will be a rainbow of colors, or maybe a color that has not yet been discovered. It could be a color that no one can ever imagine in their wildest dreams. No matter what, it is going to be beautiful."

"I hope so," said Jessica.

The next day, the desert ended, and they scaled a mountain. It was a giant mountain, and undiscovered one, and much taller than Mount Everest. They slammed pickaxes into the smooth rock and drove hooks into the rock face to attach ropes to. It was hazardous, and they had to camp on the side of the mountain.

"Are you excited to see this flower?" asked Jessica.

"Oh, yes," replied her younger brother, who was happy to be climbing a mountain. "I think that it is going to be the biggest flower that we have ever seen. It might be so big that you can't see all of it at once. We might have to spend days looking at it. I heard that it is inside a volcano. Isn't that cool?"

"Yeah, pretty cool," said Jessica. "I hope that you are right about the flower. It would be pretty funny, though, if the flower was tiny."

"I guess," said her brother, and Jessica could tell that he did not think that would be funny.

After getting to the top of the ice-capped mountain, they started down the other side. It was almost as difficult to scale down as it was to scale up. The mountain was completely smooth, so they could slide down, but they had to use their axes to dig into the mountain as they did, or they would go too fast.

It took seven hours to slide down the mountain, and they camped at the bottom before they navigated through the swamp the next day. It was nice to sit by the fire after two days of climbing up and down the mountain, and they all sang songs as the fire crackled.

In the morning, they set off through the swamp. It bubbled up around them, and noxious gas came out. Jessica thought about throwing up a few times, but she managed to save herself from doing so.

They had to walk through the swamp as there was no way to go around it. The mud under the water stuck to the bottom of their boots, and they had to really pull up their feet to move forward. Each time they took a step, they would hear a big squelch.

There was the smell too. It was awful, like stinky cheese that has been left in the toilet.

"What do you think the flower will smell like?" asked Jessica, trying to take her mind off of the smell.

"It will smell terrific," said her uncle. He twisted his mustache, getting mud all over it. "I do not think that it will smell like anything that we have smelled before. You might not understand this, but I think that it will smell like my childhood."

"I understand," said Jessica. She did not understand, but it made her uncle smile, and she was happy about that. Jessica hoped that it didn't smell like her childhood. Her childhood smelled like a rotten swamp. She presumed that her uncle had never squelched through a rotten swamp as a child.

When they finally got out of the swamp, they washed up as best they could, and camped at the bottom of the volcano. The flower was inside.

"We have to time it right," said her father. "The flower will only bloom when the moon is full. Also, there is a 79% chance that the volcano will erupt tomorrow."

They all went to sleep, hoping that the volcano would not erupt while they were in their tents. Thankfully, it did not, though it was making a lot of noise when they got up in the morning, and it was threatening to erupt.

Once more, they scaled the side of a mountain, though this one was also a volcano. When they got to the top, they all looked in at the molten lava below. They waited for the moon to start to rise as the lava bubbled and became more heated. They all crossed their fingers that it would not erupt when they were inside of it.

When the moon was almost full, they attached the ropes to the mouth of the volcano and headed for the small spot of green below. They could not see from the top how big it was.

When they got to it, they could see that it was the same size as a dollar, but round instead of flat.

"Are you sure that this is it?" asked Jessica's uncle.

"This is definitely it," said her father. "We just have to wait for it to bloom. It is going to be spectacular."

The moonlight slowly made its way into the bubbling volcano and, when it hit the green bulb, the flower began to bloom. It shed the green and showed all of its glory.

The flower was very small, almost so small that you could not see it. It was also devoid of all color. It was a dull grey that could not be duller if it tied. Jessica's uncle leaned in close and smelled it.

"There is no smell," he said.
The entire family looked at the flower, a once in a lifetime opportunity, and then looked at each other.

"Shall we go home?" asked her father.

"Yes," said everyone.

The Labyrinth

Rocco looked into the labyrinth. The entrance was boring, but he knew that the labyrinth held many secrets.

He also knew the difference between a labyrinth and a maze. A Maze had an entrance and an exit. The goal of a maze was to get from the entrance to the exit. A labyrinth had one entrance and no exit. The goal of a labyrinth was to get to the center of the labyrinth and find whatever was there, usually treasure.

It had been a right of passage for everyone in his village to go into the labyrinth and get to the center. Only then would you truly be a Minotaurus. Rocco was sure that this meant there was a Minotaur somewhere in the labyrinth. A Minotaur is a beast that is half-bull and half-human. The bottom half is a bull, and the top half is human.

"Do you know," said Rocco to the guard on the gate, "that if you are ever lost in a maze, you can place your right hand on the wall and keep your hand on the wall, following the maze until you get to an entrance or an exit. It works every time."

"Hey, quit stalling," said the guard. "Either enter the labyrinth or...hey, I didn't know that. It really works?"

"Every time," said Rocco.

"Well, I'll be," said the guard. "Now, get in there." He gave Rocco a kick, sending him into the labyrinth.

Rocco had studied for this. Studied and trained.

His studying had told him that there was a test somewhere in the labyrinth. He did not know what to expect, but he knew that it was something that would help to make him into a better person.

His training had told him that there might be some danger. He had learned to use his agility to jump large distances, he could run really far, he was also fast. They had done a lot of sprint training, so there would definitely be something to run away from.

Will I have to run from the Minotaur, wondered Rocco.

He knew that Minotaurs were strong and fast, but there were also clever. And, while the top half was human, they did have horns on their heads. The threat of a horn sticking into his bum was enough motivation to run as fast as he could.

He was so lost in thought that he almost fell into the pit. He swung his arms as he almost stepped over the edge, just keeping his balance. At the bottom of the pit was a small pond of foul-smelling goo. It looked so sticky that he was not sure that he would get out.

Rocco took a few steps back and ran towards the pit. When he got to the edge, he stepped to the side and ran along the wall, using his speed to propel himself forward. He dived and rolled at the other side, landing perfectly.

"I need to pay more attention," he said to himself.

He did pay more attention, and his studying paid off. When he found a wall full of words, he could translate them all. They were in the old languages; Latin, Greek, Viking runes. They all said the same thing. They all said, 'Duck!'

Rocco was sure that they were not talking about the semi-aquatic animal, and he almost laughed to himself at the thought of ducks attacking. He was so caught up in his own little world that he almost forgot to duck.

A large cushion, attached to a massive chain, swung through the air like a giant pendulum. Rocco's reflexes kicked in, and he was able to duck just in time. The pillow would have thrown him across the labyrinth.

"Pillows are soft," Rocco said to no one. "They certainly are soft, but I have been in my fair share of pillow fights to know ho much they can hurt when they whack you in the head."

Rocco continued on but vowed to take the labyrinth more seriously. Twice, he had almost fell victim to a trap through his own foolishness.

"Let's do this," said Rocco.

After walking for twenty minutes, he started to feel hungry. He could not believe his eyes when he saw a table packed with cakes and candy. The pile was so high that he was sure people would be able to see it from outside of the labyrinth.

There was also a sign in the table that read:

Please eat the cake and candy. They are definitely not poisoned, and in no way will they send you to sleep for two days. Completely normal candy and cakes, oh yes, yes sir, nothing suspect here, just go ahead and eat them.

Rocco decided not to eat anything, which was a good decision as they were all filled with sleeping powder. If he had eaten anything, he would have been put to sleep for two days.

Rocco felt hungry as he walked through the labyrinth, but he was too strong to give in. He knew that once he left the labyrinth, he would have a large feast waiting for him. His older sister had made it through the labyrinth, his mother and father also. All of his grandparents had made it through, and he was going to make it through too.

"Where are you, Minotaur?" asked Rocco. For a brief moment, he felt brave, even though he had nothing to protect himself with.

That moment disappeared when he reached the center of the labyrinth. There, in the middle of the labyrinth, was the Minotaur. He stood, staring at Rocco. Rocco could see that there was nothing else there, no treasure, nothing. Just the Minotaur.

There was an assortment of weapons on the wall to his left and the wall to his right. Rocco was afraid. The Minotaur was bigger than anything he had ever seen before, and muscular too. He did not think that he could defeat the beast.

He looked the Minotaur in the eyes, and looked back to the weapons, checking each one. There were swords, axes, shields, maces, and every other weapon you could imagine. Rocco looked back at the Minotaur and made his choice.

Rocco walked forward empty-handed.

"Welcome, Rocco," said the Minotaur. He bowed to Rocco.

"Thank you," said Rocco as he bowed back.

"Why did you not attack me?" asked the Minotaur.

"I didn't want to," replied Rocco. "You have never done me any harm, and I have come into your labyrinth unannounced. Why should I harm you? I was scared of you because I have never seen you before, but that is no reason to attack. When I thought about it, I decided that it would be better to meet you. I should not be scared of you because you are different."

"You are wise, Rocco," said the Minotaur. "Your wisdom will serve you well in the world. It is a pleasure to meet you, and you may come back any time to talk with me, but, for now, you must go."

"Why?" asked Rocco. "Is it dangerous here."

"Not at all," said the Minotaur. "Your feast and your family are waiting, and you must be famished."

Rocco had to admit that he was very hungry. He said goodbye to the Minotaur and left the labyrinth through the secret tunnel. His family was waiting for him, and they all gave him big hugs. They also had a feast waiting, and Rocco had never enjoyed his food more than he did after escaping the labyrinth.

The Story Of Sleep

Once upon a time, a long, long time ago, there was no sleep.

Can you imagine that? There was no sleep in the entire world.

When night came, people continued to do what they did during the day. Some people worked, others played, and some spent time with their families. But, most found that they daydreamed. They would sit during the night and daydream. When they did, they all felt a little better.

But, for the most part, people felt bad. There was something missing from their lives, and they did not know what.

It was the king who finally helped to solve the problem, though not for the reasons that you might think. He was bored with nighttime. All of the cool things happened during the day, and it was always dark at night. It was harder to play sports, people daydreamed a lot (or should that be night dreamed?), and people always seemed to be busy.

The king wished for it to be day all of the time.

So, he went to his scientists.

"When the sun goes down, the day is done," said the king. "I want you to stop the sun from going down so that it can be day all of the time, then the fun will never end."

The scientists went to work. They had many ideas, as many scientists do, and set to work trying to keep the sun in the sky for longer.

They tried to create a big net to catch the sun, but could not create one that was big enough. The tried to build a tower under the sun to stop it from moving, but could not get planning permission. They even tried asking the sun to stop moving, but the sun did not listen to them.

When they went back to the king, they told him, "We cannot stop the sun from moving."

"Hmm," said the king. "Well, if you cannot stop the day from leaving, can we time travel?"

"What do you mean?" asked the scientists.

"What if you create a machine that time travels to the future? When the moon rises, we can jump into the time machine and travel to the future, when the sun is rising again. That way, we can skip the night altogether."

"An interesting idea," said the scientists. They set to work building a time machine but found that it was impossible to do, and they could only make time *seem* to move faster. They found that when they were doing something fun, it felt like time was moving faster. And, when they were doing something boring, it felt like time slowed down.

But, no matter what they did, they could not travel through time.

"What about a fake sun?" asked the king. "We could pretend that it is still day by shining a big light over the world, and then it would be day all the time."

So, the scientists got back to work.

They built the biggest light that people had ever seen and shone it over the world. At night, it was turned on, and during the day, it was switched off. And, for a brief time, the king was happy.

For a time, everyone was happy. But, they found that it was harder to daydream. They also found that everything became more difficult. They felt more and more tired. Still, the King continued to shine the light, thinking that he was doing something good for his kingdom.

A knock soon came at the castle door, and three wise men were shown into the castle. They met with the king.

"You have created an imbalance," said the wise man of the body.

"You cannot un-split day and night," said the wise man of the mind.

"We will teach you our secrets," said the wise man of emotions.

"Your secrets," said the king.

"You were misinformed," said the wise man of the mind. "Time travel is possible, but not the way in which you think. We are here to teach you how to time travel through the night so that you can do as much as you can through the day."

"By resting," said the wise man of emotions, "you can function better."

"Teach me, teach me," said the king.

So, the three wise men taught the king all that they knew.

"First, you must rest your body," said the wise man of the body. "This is the easiest part, but you must practice it a lot."

The wise man of the body instructed the king in what he needed to do. He showed the king how to lie on a comfortable surface, and let go of all the tension in his body. The king did what the wise man said, filling a large bag with hay, and lying on top of it.

For a week, the king did this, lying perfectly still for eight hours every night, until he could do it without moving his body. On the seventh night, he found that his body would sometimes move by itself. He also felt very rested after seven nights, though he was very bored too. It is hard to lay still when you cannot do anything.

"Good," said the wise man of the body. "You have mastered the first step."

"Now, you must master the next," said the wise man of the mind. "For seven more nights, you must do the same, but you must clear your mind."

The wise man of the mind instructed the king on how to empty his mind of everything. The king tried as hard as he could. Every night, he got onto his hay pile, did not move his body, and tried to empty his mind.

As the week went on, he got better and better. On the first night, he could not help but think how silly this all was. On the third night, he thought about everything he wanted to be doing. On the fifth night, he thought about what he wanted to do with his life. And, on the seventh night, he thought about nothing. His mind was completely blank.

"Good," said the wise man of the mind.

"But I felt so bored," admitted the king.

"That is where I come in," said the wise man of emotion. "Now, you must learn the final step in this process."

"Teach me," said the king. He had to admit that he had never felt more rested.

"You must do the same as before. You must let your body rest, and you must let your mind empty of thought, but you must also hold onto any emotions that you have had throughout your day. When you hold these emotions in your mind, do not think of what happened, think about the feeling."
The king did as he was instructed. This was the hardest part of the process.

For the first few nights, he thought about the good things that had happened and could see them in his mind. He also thought of the bad things and lived them over and over. He felt angry.

On the fifth night, he could feel all the emotions well, but he could still picture the incidents in his mind. He saw them from different angles, watching himself in the images.

On the seventh night, he finally let go. He held the emotion in his body, but he did not hold the pictures in his mind.

On the seventh night, he finally dreamed.

"That was amazing," said the king when he woke up the next day. "I feel so rested."

"We have taught you our secrets," said the three wise men. "It is now time for us to go. You must teach everyone to travel through the night."

The king agreed, and he taught everyone how to sleep and dream.

From Red To Green

Sometimes it is hard to move from red to green. Have you ever tried? Do you even know what I am talking about?

Red is when you are angry. If you are angry and annoyed about something, if you have so much pent up frustration that you think that you are going to explode, then you are in the red zone.

It is easy to get into the red zone, and it can be tricky to get out of it. You do not even have to do anything to get into it, and it can take over your mind.

Almost anything can get you into the red zone. Maybe you did not get to do what you wanted to do today. Perhaps you played a game and had no luck at all. Did you fall over when you were playing sport and missed scoring a point for your team?

Lots of things can get you into the red zone, and that is okay because I'll tell you a little secret. Adults get into the red zone all of the time. The trick is to get out of the red zone. Once you know how to get out of the red zone, you can do it all of the time, and you can even teach adults to do it.

But, it does take a lot of practice.

So, if you want to get out of the red zone, where do you go?

You go to the green zone.
But what is the green zone?

The green zone is the place where you are calm and happy. You are not angry there. You are peaceful and serene. It is the exact opposite of the red zone.

It is the feeling that you have when you are just falling asleep and do not have a care in the world. It is like having a warm blanket wrapped around you, or a hug from your family. It is the feeling you get when you watch the ocean waves lapping on the beach, or listen to the sound of a river.

When you are in the green zone, you are happy and calm.

Wouldn't you like to be in the green zone instead of the red zone?

Sometimes it is not so easy. When you are in the red zone, it is hard to leave. When you are in the red zone, sometimes you do not want to leave. Sometimes you want to stay there forever.

That is why you have to practice getting out of the red zone before you even get there. When you practice it over and over, you will be able to get out of the red zone easily when you are there.

So, what can you do?

Here are some exercises to practice to get from the red zone to the green zone. The more that you practice them, the better you will get. Let's practice some of them now.

First, we are going to squeeze some lemons. Why lemons? I don't really know, by they are as good a thing as any. Of course, we are not using real lemons. We are using imaginary lemons.

So, close your eyes and imagine that you have lemons in your hands, one in each. They are slightly cool to touch, and they have bumpy skin. Hold one in each hand, and start to squeeze them.

When you are doing this, actually tense your hands and pretend that you are squeezing real lemons. Feel the skin tearing and the juice coming out. If you destroy these ones, move onto some more lemons and squeeze them too. Squeeze as many lemons as you like, or until you start to feel more green than red.

Now, when you get into the red zone, you can squeeze lemons to get you back to the green zone.

Our second method is to have an angry dance party.

You might not want to do this now if you are calmly in bed, but you can practice it in the morning if you like. All you are going to do is to put on some music, a little louder than usual, and dance to it.

Now, you want something with a little bit of a beat to it so you can dance quickly and angrily. You do not want to damage anything or anyone, so make sure that there is nothing in the way if you want to flail your arms around.

Dance for as long as you can. Dance quickly and angrily. When you are having your angry dance party, try to use the same songs too. This will help you when you are in the red zone.

So, when you do get into the red zone, you can switch on that music and start dancing to it. When you are tired out, flop down on the couch or your bed and get your breath back.

The next tool that you will use is writing and drawing, and you do not need to be any good at either to do this. All you have to do is try, and you will help yourself to feel better. Moving from red to green is a much more valuable skill than drawing pretty pictures, though that is fun too.

For this exercise, find a piece of paper and a pencil or pen. You are going to write down exactly how you feel. If you do not feel angry right now, think about a time that you were, and write down how you felt. If you are not yet great at printing on paper, or if you do not want to, you can draw how you feel.

When you draw, you do not need to draw a picture if you do not want to. You can draw a color that shows how you feel or scribbles that represent your anger. Draw exactly how you feel without thinking about it.

When you are done writing or drawing, you can show a parent or guardian if you want. If you want to talk about it, you can. If you do not want to talk about it, you do not have to.

If you are still feeling angry after writing or drawing, then tear up the paper. Go ahead, rip it into as many pieces as you want and throw it up in the air (make sure to clean up when you are back in the green zone).

When you get into the red zone, pull out some paper and pencils, and show how you are feeling.

These tools take time and practice to master. That is why you need to practice them when you are in the green zone, and you are calm and happy.

The more you practice, the more you will be able to do them when you are in the red zone. Do not worry if you cannot do them every time, the red zone is a tough place to be, but the more you try, the more it will happen.

The red zone is not a bad place, it is just a place where our emotions are, and that makes us who we are. Everyone gets angry, even those people in your family. Once you can master the red zone, you will become a better person.

For now, it is time to sleep (unless you are reading this during the day. If you are, then now is the time to practice).

Well done for listening to or reading this story. It is the first step in your journey from the red zone to the green zone, and your first step to becoming a better person.

The Wind

The wind can come in many forms. Sometimes it comes to us in tiny little wisps that blow through our hair, lifting it slightly. Those tiny zephyrs of air like to play with the leaves in the trees, or stir up those on the ground.

Sometimes, the wind blows a little harder. That kind of wind is amazing when you are riding your bike or playing soccer. It helps to cool you, especially when you are really sweaty. This is the kind of wind that likes to lift plastic bags from the garbage and toss them in the air, making them dance.

Then, there is the wind that is a little louder. This wind can be hard to walk through. When it comes at night, it can make funny noises as it rushes past your home, noises like an elephant trumping or a witch whistling.

The last type of wind is the wind that you do not want to be caught in. It can swirl in large circles and lift houses from the ground. Thankfully, that wind does not come very often.

The wind can be gentle, and it can be tough, just like you. The wind also likes to travel. Every day, the wind travels around the entire world. It sees so many amazing people and things. Every day, it visits you. The wind thinks that you are pretty amazing.

What does the wind see as it travels around the world?

There are too many amazing things to count, but here are some of them.

Though the wind cannot get underwater very easily, it can stir up the water. When the wind travels over Australia, it likes to stay still and calm the water so that it can see the Great Barrier Reef.

The Great Barrier Reef is underwater and is a living thing. It is made out of coral and houses lots of different animals. Lots of fish live there, along with dolphins and whales. It stretches for more than 3,000 kilometers. That might be even bigger than the country that you live in. There are even turtles and sea snakes that live there.

The Great Wall of China is another place that the wind likes to blow over. The wall is strong, so the wind does not have to worry about being calm. Did you know that the Great Wall of China was built over 2,000 years ago? That is a very long time ago.

When it was built, it was created to stop people from invading and attacking. Thankfully, there are no attackers anymore, and people can even walk on top of the wall. Yes, it is wide enough to walk on top of it!

In India, there is a beautiful palace. It is called the Taj Mahal. It is one of the most beautiful buildings in the world, and the wind can blow all around without damaging it. It was created as a present from a man to a woman. He built it to show how much he loved her.

When the wind gets to America, it heads straight for the Grand Canyon. It is fun to blow over the land, and move across dusty plains or up mountains, but you can make really cool noises if you blow through crevices or valleys. The Grand Canyon has lots of valleys.

If you were to try and hike through the Grand Canyon, it would take you a lot of time to get from one end to the other. The valleys are deep, and there are rivers that run through it. It can also get really hot. But, that is no problem for the wind, and it likes to go there to play.

There are many waterfalls in the world, and the one that the wind likes best is the Iguaza falls in Brazil and Argentina. If you have ever seen a waterfall, then you know how cool they can be, but I bet that you have never seen a waterfall that is as big as this!

The waterfall is so loud that you might not even be able to hear the wind when you are there. The wind likes to go there, even if it cannot be heard sometimes. The thing it likes most about going to Iguaza falls is making the water dance. As the water falls, it is fun to blow it across the sky.

The Sagrada Familia in Spain is a building like no other that you will ever see, and the wind likes to go there and perch in the trees beside it. Sometimes the wind will just sit there and take in the beauty of the building. The building is known as a Basilica and was designed by a famous artist, Antoni Gaudi. He never got to finish it, and people are still building parts of it today, even though it was started over a hundred years ago.

The Scottish Highlands are an amazing place to go if you want some peace and quiet, as long as you don't mind the sound of sheep and, of course, and the wind. The wind loves to go there, and I know this because the Scottish Highlands can be a very windy place.

They are beautiful too. There are large stony mountains, rolling green hills, purple heather, thistles, and lots of animals. The wind likes to tickle the fur and hair of the animals. There are stags, sheep, highland cows, otters, beavers, mice, birds, and more. If you are very sneaky, you might even see a haggis running around too. The wind has seen one, or so it tells me.

The wind also likes to visit the places where no people live, like deserted islands and places where it is very cold. Of course, some people live in the cold, but most do not. The wind visits all of the places where there are only animals.

There are some islands where only penguins live, or where seals hunt, or where walruses bask, or where dolphins and whales swim. Sometimes there are sea lions, and giant tortoises, and marine iguanas, and wonderful birds and fish. The wind loves every living being on earth.

The wind also goes to Mount Everest and sits on top of the world. From up there, it can see everything, and it can blow as hard as it wants without damaging anything. Of course, sometimes there are visitors at the top of Mount Everest, and the wind tries not to blow so hard, but it gets excited often and cannot help it.

The deserts are also fun to visit. There are not usually too many people there, so it can blow as hard as it wants, and sand is very fun to blow around. Have you ever played with sand? It is fun, right? The wind likes to blow it around and create shapes. There are lots of sand dunes in the desert, large piles of sand, and that is all created by the wind.

Blowing all day is hard work, so sometimes, the wind does not blow at all. When it has a lot of energy, it will blow a lot and, when it is tired, it will stop. If you were the wind, where would you travel to, and who would you visit?

It is hard work being the wind. There is always something to do and somewhere to go. The wind is always traveling, seeing everything and everyone that the world has to offer, and that includes you.

So, the next time that you feel the wind on your face, or your hair is lifted, or a breeze ruffles your clothes, know that it is the wind just come to visit. If you have the time, make sure to wave to the wind and say hello.

When The Moon Disappeared

Luna perched on the top of the craggy rock, looking down below. There had been some talk of wolves in the area, and she was there to make sure that they did not get too close to her village. She was the head of the elf scouts and always made sure that the rest of the elves in her village were taken care of.

"Something feels weird," she said to Barko.

Barko was her second in command and the nicest elf that anyone had ever met. But, you would not know that to look at him. He stood almost a foot taller than any other elf and had a scar on his cheek. He had got that scar when he fell off his bike as a child, but everyone thought that he got it in battle.

While Luna was not as tall as Barko, she was just as fierce. She could use her words to get things done, and she was the smartest elf in the village. That was why she was the leader of the elf scours and tasked with protecting the village.

"What do you think it is?" asked Barko.

"I don't know," said Luna. "Just feels off, like something is about to happen."

They looked to the distance and could see wolves there, but the wolves were running away from the village. Luna did not think that her village was under any danger, but she was still wary. She tugged on her pointy ears, as she always did when she was deep in thought, and whistled an elven tune.

"What did the village elder say?" asked Luna.

"Only that hard times were coming. That the wolves and the water would be affected," replied Barko.

"The wolves and the water. What could that be? Maybe she was wrong," suggested Luna, touching the arrows on her back. She was an amazing shot with her bow and arrow.

"She's never been wrong before," said Barko.

"That's true," responded Luna.

They descended into silence, listening only to the sound of the crickets chirping in the darkness. Luna looked all around her, everything beautiful and basked in moonlight. She tried to think about what could affect the wolves and the water.

Her eyes widened in surprise as it came to her, though she was still skeptical about the entire thing. She suddenly looked up, and Barko looked up to. They both stared at the moon.

"The moon," they said together.

As they said it, almost as if they had triggered the event, the moon began slowly shrinking. It got smaller and smaller until it was only a dot in the sky, and then it disappeared.

Luna and Barko looked at each other. This was a serious issue, and it had to be fixed, but they did not know how. There was nothing to do right now, so they returned to their village and slept.

In the morning, they told everyone what they had seen. A village meeting was called, but no one knew what to do about it. Even the village elders had to think more about the issue. Luna decided to talk to the ones who might know something.

"Come on, Barko," she said. "We have some investigating to do.

They made the trip through the forest and across the plains until they came to the ocean. When they got there, they could see that the ocean had been crying. It was sitting where it normally sat, but it was not moving. The ocean was depressed.

"Oh, Great Ocean," said Luna. "We have come for your help. The moon has disappeared, and we do not know what to do."

"You do not know what to do!" boomed the ocean. "Look at me! What am I going to do?"

"Can we help?" asked Luna.

"No one can help me," said the ocean. "My tides have gone. I always worked in harmony with the moon, my tides would ebb and flow. It would make me happy, the beach would be happy, the sea creatures would be happy, and everyone else would be happy."

"I have found a lot of joy watching your waves and tides," said Barko. "I always came here as a young boy."

"Well, now that is gone," said the ocean. "The moon is gone forever."

"Is it really gone?" asked Luna.

"I think so," said the ocean. "I can still remember the moon, but it is like a distant memory. I cannot help you."

Luna and Barko left the ocean to be sad. They did not know what they could do to help it, but they had to try. They went to visit the wolves next.

The elves and the wolves had never been friends, but there had always been a respect between them. When Luna and Barko got close to the wolf village, they expected some warning growls, but there were none. When they entered the village, the wolves were lazing around, lying on the ground.

"What happened?" asked Luna.

"There is no point to anything anymore," said a wolf.

"What do you mean?" asked Luna.

"If there is no moon to howl at, then what point in life is there. We have always howled at the moon, but not the moon is gone," said the wolf.

"Can you not howl at something else?" asked Barko.
"How dare you!" growled the wolf. "We cannot go around just howling at anything. We have howled at the moon for centuries. We're not animals!"

The wolf walked off.

"I hope that it returns," muttered an old wolf who was standing close to them.

"What do you mean?" asked Luna.

"Please, just leave us," said the old wolf. "We are in too much pain to have this stirred up."

Luna and Barko agreed to leave, but something was stirring inside of Luna. When she got back to the village, she shared her finings with the other elves.

"I have a feeling that the moon is gone, but not forgotten. I think that it is still out there, and the ocean and wolves can still feel it," said Luna.

"Hmm," said an elder. "Then we may be able to bring it back."

"We have been studying the old texts," said another of the elders. "It seems that the moon would often travel when it did not feel needed anymore. It would only come back after a number of years, but we can perform the moon dance to bring it back. If we show the moon that it is loved, we can bring it back."

"What do we need to do?" asked Luna.

The preparations were made, and everyone in the village was outside as the night fell. Without the moon, there was not as much light as there used to be, and large fires had to be lit.

The elders gave out the instructions.

As large drums were beaten, the elves gathered in large circles, dancing with hands linked, around and around in the shape of the moon.

They broke hands and held their arms out, waving them from side to side like the tides. A strange wind blew over the village, and Luna was sure that she could hear the ocean's sound. She was convinced that the ocean was dancing too.

When the water part was done, everyone shook their bodies and took in a large breath of air. Still shaking their bodies, they let out a large howl, pointing it upwards towards the sky. One, two, three times they did it, but nothing happened.

Then, there was another howl. The wolves had joined in, howling for the moon to return. As the wolves howled, the ocean moved, and the people danced, the moon could see how much it was missed, and returned to shine on the world.

Every year after that, on the same day the moon first disappeared, the elves all gathered to dance the dance of the moon. The ocean and the wolves joined in too, and the moon never disappeared again.

The Luckiest Boy In The World

John did not know it when he was born, but he was destined to become the luckiest boy in the world.

Even the story of his birth is quite lucky. His parents were hiking in Peru, halfway up a mountain, hundreds of miles away from any other people, and a great distance from any hospitals when John decided it was time to be born.

Now, you might be thinking that it was a silly decision to go hiking so far from anywhere when you are pregnant, and you would be right, but John's mom and dad were searching for a lost city, and it was still a week before he was due to be born, so they did not think that anything bad would happen.

They were wrong.

Just as they discovered a building from the lost village, only the second time it had ever been discovered in history, John's mom started to give birth.

This would have been a big problem if John was not so lucky.

As his parents ran into the building to find somewhere soft to rest, they discovered some doctors and nurses who just happened to be taking a vacation with all of their medical equipment (they were the first people in history to discover this lost village).

"Well, this is certainly lucky," said the doctor, who had, for some reason, just washed and sanitized her hands in case she was needed.

"Yes," said the nurses, who had only just finished setting up a comfortable bed in case someone would need it.

The birth went without a hitch. There was even lots of green clover around, which was even luckier, especially as it was not supposed to grow there.

As John grew up, he got luckier and luckier.

There was one time, and one time only, that he was bullied. Well, someone tried to bully him, but they never tried again.

John was standing beside a stream, and an older boy walked past, thinking that it would be funny to kick John in. John was facing the water, so he did not see the kick coming, but he did move out of the way just in time, distracted by a rare silver and pink butterfly. The older boy splashed straight into the stream.

Well, the older boy was so annoyed that he decided to give John a wedgie. He ran after John, trying to pull John's underwear up at the back so that it would really hurt, and John was too busy not walking under a ladder to notice this older boy.

Through some strange turn of events, that I won't even try to describe here because they are too indescribable, the older boy managed to give himself a wedgie, kick himself in the shin, and then hang himself in a tree.

When John finally turned around, he saw the boy hanging in the tree and helped him down. The older boy was very grateful, and John was never bullied from that day. Not that anyone would be able to if they tried.

There was also the big soccer game. His school team was in the final of the biggest tournament in the country. They were not the best team, but they did have a lot of luck. John's team was trailing by two goals with only one minute to go.

The other team was attacking, and, for some reason, John decided to kick the ball towards his own goal. The goalkeeper dived for the ball and missed it. The ball hit the post and rebounded all the way to the other end of the field, going straight into the other goal. The other goalkeeper had been paying so little attention that he did not even notice the ball trickle past him.

He paid more attention when the game restarted with forty seconds to go, but could not stop the ball the next time. The other team kicked off and booted the ball. It somehow hit John's bum, flew up the field, and looped over the goalkeeper. He could do nothing to stop it.

When the game kicked off again with ten seconds to go, the other team tried to hold onto the ball but, through events that are not even worth describing, the ball ended up in their goal again through sheer luck. John's team had won.

Don't even get me started on the time he managed to score two baskets at the same time with one ball in basketball or how he managed to score nine home runs with one hit in baseball.

Any game that John plays, he wins, so do not play games with him. There are also some games that he was won by not playing. There was a marathon too. He ran away from an angry dog one time and ended up running an entire marathon, winning it by more than seven minutes.

When he was five, he got into a bike accident and almost joined the circus. He was riding his bike in a field, close to a place where there was a circus, but he had no idea of this. He rode his bike quickly down a hill, and, when he hit the bottom, his wheel got stuck in a hole, and he went flying over the handlebars.

He would have hit the ground it someone had not left a trampoline in the exact spot that he was due to land. After bouncing on the trampoline, he landed in a circus canon. That cushioned his fall, and everything would have been fine if it had not been for his momentum.

The cannon was pointing away from the circus tent. Still, the momentum shifted the cannon so that it pointed directly toward the tent. A small campfire that had just been lit, and unattended for exactly nine seconds, lit the cannon fuse and sent John flying through the air again.

He thought that he was done for this time as he headed toward the large canvas tent. The wind blew and opened a small slit in the tent, where the stitches had come away. It was just big enough for John to fit through.

If the trapeze artist had jumped at the right time, there would be no one to catch John, but she had felt her lace come undone and bent down to tie it. That was when John flew over her shoulder and across the circus tent. The man on the other trapeze caught him, and he looked as surprised as John did.

The crowd went wild, and John was offered a job in the circus. He declined. He was only five, and he would much rather go to school. School would be much more fun than the circus. And it was. John got up to so many fun and lucky things in school that I would have to write an entire book just to describe them.

One of those things included becoming a teacher for the day, and the other included saving the school from dinosaurs, but you probably don't want to hear about that.

Anyway, what would you do if you were as lucky as John? If you could drink a magic potion or have a magic spell cast on you, and you would become the luckiest person in the world for one day, what would you do?

I hope that, as you go to sleep tonight, you dream of all the things that you would do.

Goodnight.

Survival

"I'm going out," said Amy.

"Have fun," said her parents.

Amy was only eight years old, but she was independent and feisty. She loved to learn new things, and always wanted to learn new skills. One of her favorite things to do was to go outside with her friends and pretend that they were camping out in an inhospitable climate.

An inhospitable climate is a place where it is difficult to live. When you live in a place like that, you have to do all that you can to survive.

Amy's friends were all busy today, so she headed off into the small woods by herself. She could have lots of fun on her own.

She had her bag with her, and, in that bag, she had packed all of the essentials. She had some string, a flashlight, a warm hat, flint and steel, her stuffed bunny, Hopsy, two granola bars, an apple, some water, a small knife, and zip ties. It was all she would need should she be lost in an inhospitable environment.

As Amy walked into the woods, she got completely lost. She had been in the woods many times before, and she had never got lost, but this time she did.

"Okay, I have to survey my surroundings," she said.

She was good at survival, and she knew that she had to get the lie of the land before she did any planning. She found a good climbing tree, one with lots of branches, and climbed to the top. When she got there, she checked all around her.

On one side, there was an ocean, mountains were on another, the forest stretched as far as she could see in another direction, and a swamp made up the rest. She even brought Hopsy from the bag to confirm what she saw. He confirmed it with a nod.

She was sleepy by this time, so she thought it best to make a shelter where she could sleep. At the base of the tree, she gathered thick branches and placed them up against it. After that, she placed smaller branches and leaves on top, finishing it off with moss.

It was a very nice shelter, and she placed Hopsy in it to look after it while she went off in search of food. She found some berries close by and came back to camp. When she returned, she took the flint and steel from her bag. She could use them to make some fire.

She gathered some large logs, put small ones on top, and topped that with dry leaves and kindling. She used the flint and steel to make a spark. There was soon a roaring fire. Amy and Hopsy ate berries while the fire crackled.

When she was a little more tired, Amy retreated to the enclosure. Hopsy stayed by the fire to keep a lookout. When Amy woke, the fire had gone out, and Hopsy was fast asleep.

"Great lookout, you are," she said to Hopsy, nudging him with her foot.

Amy had thought that someone might come looking for her, but they had not. They would have to spend more time in the wilderness.

"More food," said Amy as her stomach rumbled.

There was only one thing to do. She would have to build a raft and go fishing in the ocean. She packed up her stuff and walked to the shore. When she got there, she found some nice logs and bound them together with string and zip ties to make a raft.

She found a piece of wire and bent it into a hook, tying some string to it. All she needed now was some bait. Digging a big hole helped her to discover lots of worms. She put one worm on the hook and ate one, popping it in her mouth and chewing on it. She was really hungry. Hopsy ate one too.

She pushed the raft out, hopped on, and dropped the hook into the water. It did not take long for her to catch a rainbow fish, catfish, and flying fish. Back at the shore, she started another fire, and she and Hopsy ate the fish while looking out over the waves.

"We need to find our way home, Hopsy," said Amy. She did not think that anyone was out looking for her. "Animals are smart, we should follow one."

Amy was very good at tracking animals, especially rabbits. Hopsy was a rabbit, and she had spent a lot of time with him. She did not find any rabbit tracks, but she did find a deer track and possibly a coyote footprint.

She followed the deer prints through the forest. They took her away from the ocean and deeper into the trees. When she came out on the other side, there were no deers, but there were penguins. They were all very cute.

Amy was glad that she had packed her warm hat and put it on before she froze. She took a sip from her bottle of water, saving some for later. It was always wise to ration food and water, and that was why she had not eaten her granola bars yet.

"Do you know the way to go, penguins?" asked Amy.

The penguins honked at her, but she did not speak penguin, so she had no idea what they were saying. She walked past them and continued up the snowbank, hoping to find a landmark that she would use. She had a vague idea of what her house looked like, and was sure that she would recognize it when she saw it.

When she got to the top of the snowbank, she only saw a desert beyond it. She thought that it was weird for a snow tundra and a desert to be side by side, but she decided not to question it, she had other things to worry about.

When she was in the desert, she thought about taking off the hat, but it was smarter to keep it on. It would make her hotter, but it would save her from burning. And, she had saved lots of water, so she was sure that she could make it through.

"Be brave," she said to Hopsy.

Some sand snakes soon appeared, but she tied them together with zip ties so that they could not bite her. Luckily, she found a camel soon after that, and the camel let her ride on its back. That helped her to get through the desert, and she was soon on the other side.

When she reached the volcano, she hoped that she was going the right way. She knew that she could not go back, so she scaled it instead. At the top, she found a cave full of treasure. There was gold, and diamonds, and other precious gems. There was also a dragon in there too.

The dragon would have got her if it were not for the flashlight. She pulled it out of her pocket and shined it on the treasure. Rays of light bounced off, blinding the dragon so that they could escape. Hopsy almost got bitten.

They ran down the other side of the volcano and tumbled into a forest.

"Hey, this looks familiar," said Amy.

They walked through the forest, and Amy found her back yard. She was home! She ran through her yard and into the house.

"I'm home!" she shouted.
"Welcome home," said her mother.

"Weren't you worried?" asked Amy. "I was gone for such a long time. It must have been days. There were penguins, dragons, a volcano, swamps, trees, oceans, rafts, fires, and adventure."

"That's fun," said her mother. "I'm glad that you played outside by yourself for so long. You were gone for over an hour."

Amy folded her arms and sighed. Adults were never very good at keeping time.

Amy went back upstairs and packed her sword and shield into her bag. Next time, she would slay the dragon and take its treasure.

The Angry Crocodile

Crocodile was an angry crocodile. No one was quite sure why Crocodile was such an angry crocodile, but they knew better than to hang around when he came walking along. He was always shouting and chomping, and the other animals were scared that they would have their heads bitten off.

Bear first met Crocodile when he was fishing. Bear sat on the banks of the river, dropping his fishing line into the water, hoping to catch some fish for his dinner. He had only been there for six minutes when Crocodile appeared. It was the first and last time that Bear met Crocodile.

The crocodile came waking out of the water, gnashing his teeth, and shouting things that Bear could not make out. Bear did not waste any time. He dropped his fishing rod, knocked over his small chair, scrambled up the bank, knocking over his snacks and drinks, and ran home as fast as he could.

Bear never went back to the river again.

Most animals ran away when they saw Crocodile, but Owl tried something different. He had studied animal brains his whole life, and he was sure that Crocodile was angry because of something that had happened in his past.

Owl kept a lookout for Crocodile, and, when he saw him walking about on the banks of the river, chomping his teeth, he made his move. Owl swooped from his tree, flew close to Crocodile, and alighted on a branch in a nearby tree.

"I am here to help you," said Owl.

"Roar!" shouted Crocodile.

"Tell me about your past," said Owl.

"I was walking," said Crocodile.

"No, no," said Owl. "Tell me about your parents. What were they like? How was your childhood?"

"Can you," started Crocodile.

"Has something happened to you?" asked Owl. "Something happened in your past, didn't it, and that is why you are so angry. Share your pain with me, Crocodile."

"I was walking," said Crocodile.

"Oh, well, if you are not going to help yourself, then I cannot help you," said Owl. He flew off back to his home, chasing his head and hooting.

The next animal to try and help Crocodile was Fox. Fox had watched Owl try to help Crocodile and was sure that he had failed because Crocodile had been so angry.

"There is no point in trying to talk with him when he is so angry," said Fox to himself. "Now, to prepare."

Fox found cleaning in the forest and made it as calming as possible. He found camomile flowers and lavender. He laid them out in the clearing, and they created the most amazing smell. Fox asked the bees for some honey, and he placed a bowl of honey in the middle of the clearing. That would surely help to calm him.

He found some candles, leftovers from a human camping trip, and placed them around the clearing, though he did not light them as fire is dangerous in the forest. He also found some insects to come and hum a nice song.

When all was ready, Fox went down to the banks of the river and shouted, "Crocodile, come here! I can help you!"

It did not take long for Crocodile to come blustering from the river. He raised his front foot and waved it in the air.

"Yeah, come and get me!" shouted Fox.

Crocodile took a few steps forward and waved his foot in the air again.

"Yeah, you are so angry!" shouted Fox. "Only a little bit more, and you can get rid of your anger."

Fox continued to shout at Crocodile, while Crocodile followed and shook his foot in the air. When Fox had finally lured Crocodile to the clearing, he stood back, relaxed, and watched the results of his hard work.

Crocodile immediately destroyed everything, stomping over all of the flowers, biting the candles, and scaring the insects away. He even stuck his foot in the honey instead of eating it.

"Well, I cannot help you," complained Fox. He trotted away, shaking his head.

Tiger stood and watched the whole thing. He laughed as Fox tried to calm the crocodile.

"He doesn't need to be calmed," said Tiger. "He needs someone to show him that he is not the only angry one. I will show him that he is not alone, and, if that does not work, I will show him just how angry I can be."

Tiger wasted no time and jumped out in front of Crocodile.

"Well, you think that you are angry? Look how angry I am!" shouted Tiger. He leaped around in a circle, moving around Crocodile, as the crocodile shook honey from his foot.

"I don't know what," Crocodile started shouting, but Tiger only shouted louder.

"I don't want to hear your excuses!" shouted Tiger. "Do you think that you are the only angry one in the world? I am angry too!"

"My foot!" shouted Crocodile.

"Yes, your foot is covered in honey!" shouted Tiger. "I don't care, you did that to yourself. You think that you can be angry for no reason!"

"My foot!" shouted Crocodile again.

"Oh, be quiet about your foot!" shouted Tiger. "You think that you are angry, well I am even angrier. When I get done showing you just how angry I can be, you will never want to be angry ever again!"

Tiger roared even louder, drowning out all of Crocodile's roars and words. Tiger bounded up and down, roaring and gnashing his teeth. He swiped at trees, stomped flowers, and scared away any other animals that dared to come close.

When Tiger was done, he was out of breath, but he was proud of himself because he had helped this silly crocodile. When Crocodile roared again, Tiger lost his smile. He thought that he had helped, but he had not.

"There is no helping you," said Tiger. "If you want to be angry, then go ahead. You can be the angriest animal in the entire world, for all that I care." Tiger bounded off and never returned.

Squirrel sat on the tree branch, eating an acorn. He had watched all of the animals in turn as they tried to help Crocodile. He took another bite of the nut and sighed.

"Crocodile!" he shouted.

The crocodile looked up at the tree and chomped his teeth.

"Has anyone actually asked you why you are angry?" asked Squirrel.

"I have tried to tell them," shouted Crocodile. "I tried to ask Bear for help, but he ran away. I tried to ask Owl for help, but he only wanted to talk about my parents. I know that Fox tried to help me, and I showed him my foot, but he did not look at it. I told Tiger about my foot, but that only made him angrier. No one wants to help me."

"So, your foot is the problem?" asked Squirrel.

"Yes!" roared Crocodile. "I got a thorn stuck in it a few weeks ago, and I can't get it out. Why won't anyone help me?"

"They are too silly," said Squirrel. "Can I take a look?"

"Please!" shouted Crocodile.

Squirrel came down from his tree to take a look.

"Honey," he said.

"I thought that it would help if I dipped my foot in it," shouted Crocodile.

"I think that I see it. This might hurt a little. One, two, three!"

"Roar!" roared Crocodile.

"Got it," said Squirrel.

As soon as the thorn was out of his foot, Crocodile felt much better.

"I'm not really an angry crocodile," said Crocodile.

"Hey, anyone would be angry if they had a thorn stuck in their foot," said Squirrel.

"Thanks for helping me," said Crocodile.

"Any time," said Squirrel.

The two of them became best friends and enjoyed the rest of the honey together.

www.ingramcontent.com/pod-product-compliance
Lightning Source LLC
Chambersburg PA
CBHW071830080526
44589CB00012B/967